from the Start

Right
from the Start

Investing in parents and babies

ALAN SINCLAIR

C|C|W|B press

First published by CCWB Press in 2018
Centre for Confidence and Well-being.
Registered Office Abercorn House,
79 Renfrew Rd, Paisley, PA3 4DA

© Alan Sinclair

Cover artwork by Rhiannon Van Muysen

The moral rights of the author have been asserted.

A catalogue record of this book is available
from the British Library
ISBN 978-0-9933527-7-5

Printed and bound in Great Britain by
Airdrie Print Services.

From generation to generation,
Peter and Jenny Sinclair,
Michele Veldman,
Eva and Thomas Sinclair

POSTCARDS FROM SCOTLAND

Series editor: Carol Craig

Advisory group:
Phil Hanlon and Fred Shedden

Contents

CHAPTER ONE
Introduction

'There can be no keener revelation of a society's soul,' said Nelson Mandela, 'than the way in which it treats its children.' Nicola Sturgeon brought the message closer to home when she said: 'We want Scotland to be the best place in the world to bring up children.'

But mind the gap. UNICEF, the United Nations Children's Emergency Fund, has carried out the most robust study available on child well-being across 29 of the world's advanced economies. The UK, a decent proxy for Scotland, was scored in 16th position – below the Czech Republic, Slovenia and Ireland. At the top of the table are Holland, Norway, Iceland and Finland. We scored particularly badly in early childhood education and the number of young people not in work, training or education.

Returning from a visit to Utrecht and Amsterdam to see how they achieved this, I spoke to a Dutch woman who had spent the first half of her life in Holland and the second half in Scotland. Her view was straightforward: 'In Holland we love children. In Scotland you tolerate children.'

Surely not. Yet it is a fact that today more than one Scottish child in four arrives at primary school 'vulnerable'. Vulnerable is defined as poor in one or more of social competence, emotional maturity, language and cognitive ability or physical health and well-being. About half of the vulnerable children come from the 40% of households with the lowest income. The other half live with higher earning parents.

Some consequences are visible; disruptive kids in school and poor attainment. Others like poor physical and mental health, offending, alcohol abuse and youth unemployment are delayed. But timing should not blind us to the source of the problem. Other consequences are obscured.

Today there are 15,000 Scots children in various forms of social care. Glasgow Health and Social Care Partnership spend over half of its total budget for children's services on looking after nearly 1,350 children and young people. The annual cost is over £95m. Of that nearly £42m is spent on 239 children and young people in care – at an average cost of £175,700. Per year, per child.

Many of these children have complex needs and are traumatised by their early lives. What does this say about us as adults and as a society?

In this book I use many examples from Scotland because that is where I have lived and worked most of my life. But what I identify as the requirements for babies' and children's healthy life experiences are relevant across the UK and beyond.

All of us are ex-children, still have our childish moments and may have our own children. Yet when it comes to understanding what happens in this early period of life, we are away with the fairies. As a society we don't appreciate the benefits, or the damage, that parenting can bring upon our youngest citizens, even before they are born. We have barely started to understand the personal burdens and economic costs of unplanned pregnancies and childhood neglect and trauma. Our personal views and the views embedded in our institutions are child blind. This has a cumulative effect on each of us and on the fabric and feel of our communities.

Scientific evidence shows that the womb is by no means the safe place for babies that we traditionally imagined. The first days and months after being born have the biggest lifetime effects. Major discoveries in biological, neurological and genetic science have shown that physical, cognitive and emotional development has its foundations very, very early in life. At conception a rapidly expanding collection of cells needs a safe and nurturing home. In the womb and after birth, growth of the brain, body and behaviour is sequential with one step being the foundation for the next stage. Skipping a stage is not helpful. This critical foundation stage stretches from before conception through pregnancy till about two years of age.

This book is largely about these transformative first 1,000 days. Days that are currently overlooked and misunderstood yet make the biggest difference. Following on from these 1,000 days comes the second most important period in each of our lives. This stretches from two until about five years of age: the second 1,000 days.

Being a parent can be a rich joy that enhances the whole of life. Or it can be a shouting sterile battlefield. Like a house, babies need foundations and if those foundations are not right life is wobbly. Building a house and then trying to build or correct the foundations is a distressing and expensive mistake. You may not succeed.

Better parenting will tackle Scotland's 'intractable' problems such as violence, poor mental health, alcoholism, obesity, low productivity and inadequate school attainment. As I show these are not different problems but the same problem expressed in different ways.

Scottish parenting is not universally awful: if we were we would not be almost halfway up the global table of child well-being. Much of what we individually and collectively do as parents is good, producing happy, well-adjusted children who go on to build rewarding lives and careers. But as individuals and as a society we fall well short in appreciating and acting on the benefits and significance of the first 1,000 days.

A good news story

In Scotland we have some uncomfortable truths to confront, but nonetheless at the heart of this book is a good news story. Building a nation of better parents and happier kids is not an impossible task. There is so much we can do to influence positive change. It is not by luck that Dutch children are the happiest and have the greatest well-being in the world. It is liberating to know that improving parenting is not about tilting at windmills. There are serious practical steps that we can take both as people and as a society. On our doorstep we have fantastic models and case studies of successful child-rearing support to investigate and emulate.

Being a decent parent is not that complicated. In the era before washing machines, central heating and i-this and i-that, and when money was scarce, lots of people did a good job with their children. But many children were (and are) victims of serious inter-generational problems. In turn children from such homes frequently repeat the practices of their own parents.

Improving parenting by better preparing and supporting mothers and fathers and carers is in itself, the right thing to do. It also makes financial sense for the state and therefore for us as tax payers. Long-term analysis of data on children whom researchers have followed into adulthood in different countries shows that investing in the first and the second 1,000 days produces the best rate of return on public spend; between 7% and 10% per annum.

The financial benefits flow from reduced crime and punishment, improved health, fewer people on welfare and more people working and paying tax.

Currently Scottish public expenditure is not directed to prevention and early days. It does not therefore gain the rewards. In education, we spend most money per head at around 20 years of age on the most able people who go to university. We spend the least money on the first and second 1,000 days on babies and their most important teacher – their parents. In health we spend most money on people's final days before death, and least on looking after new parents before, during and after conception. Our priorities and spending are topsy-turvy.

Telltale signs in the maternity ward
Each week 1,000 children are born in Scotland. Let's go into the maternity ward to meet four of them. Smell the toast, dodge the helium balloons, walk round each cot and take time to observe the visiting parents, family and friends.

This first little poppet will be cared for and cherished and introduced to babyccinos. Engaged friends and family surround her.

Next door is a lad who is equally loved but there are evident domestic strains. Household cash is spent before it comes in. But the mum does a good job of looking out for him and being warm and attentive.

On the surface all seems to be in order for the third baby in the ward. She comes from a good home and her elder two siblings are doing well. But this is a new life and some babies, in a seemingly unfathomable way, do not do what you expect them to do as they grow up.

May I speak now on behalf of this little chap over here, the fourth baby in the ward; born earlier and lighter in weight than the others? He may surprise us, children often do. But more likely in time he will be defiant at primary school and hard to control. At secondary school he will be a poor achiever and graduate to a record of offending and the dole. The mum loves her baby but has spent her own young life being ignored and flung about. As for the dad, he is rarely at home as there are other places where he can fly off the handle, drink and have sex. The mother's trauma will be visited on the child. This baby boy only has one visitor.

If you could advise each of these four when they were about to be conceived, your message would be: choose your mother and father with the utmost care. If tiny babies were prudent and had enough pocket (nappy?) money they would be well advised to take out insurance against being dealt a faulty parent.

With the knowledge we have today, it is entirely possible to foresee the most likely outcomes for these wee mites as soon as they are born. At three years of age it can be predicted with even more conviction how content each will be with their life as an adult. We can also say with some certainty where each child will end up in the competition for careers. For most children fostering, adoption, kinship care, day care and primary school come too late to improve their life chances. These interventions fail to tackle the core issue: the early relationship between the mother, father or carer and the child. Parenting needs to be right first time.

No one who becomes a parent starts off with a desire to harm his or her baby. But having a child makes you no more a decent parent than having a chess set makes you a decent chess player.

Scotland is a community of intelligent citizens who want the place they live in to be better than it is. They want all children in that ward to have a fair crack at life. What would it take, in practice, to give each baby an equal opportunity to thrive? How do other nations meet this challenge much more fully than we do? And what would it take to really make Scotland one of the best countries in which to grow up?

Cultural, institutional and economic factors rob children of the appropriate attention they need and the respect they deserve. In a shared house the dirty dishes tend to gather in the sink because it is no one's responsibility to wash them. Universities, secondary and primary schools are only responsible for improving the young people once they come through their door. They are not charged with improving the behaviour or intellectual capacity of our community as a whole. The NHS is orientated to sorting technical health problems and steers away from the human and preventable.

Like the flat mates with dirty crockery, no single institution, local or central government has the responsibility to prepare and support parents, and so the collective benefits are squandered. 'It is not my job.'

Some voices have advocated a shift of national resources to parenthood and early days of life, but they are outmanoeuvred and drowned out by louder voices. As yet there is no public or political clamour to prioritise child well-being in more than a rhetorical way. Priority is given to where money has been spent before, the loudest voices, and the best connected. We are not going to see a bunch of babies and toddlers demanding better parenting or meaningful support for struggling parents.

Parenting can be wonderful but it is demanding and creates its own complications and mysteries. All parents of very young children are hungry for help. If there is a time of life when you try hardest to change old patterns it is when you have a child. Supporting parents-to-be and parents makes sense when public spending is in short supply. Human and financial benefits will come from better prediction, prevention and early intervention – all with the child-parent relationship at the centre.

Some people worry that the Nanny State will take over family life. The only place where that currently happens is in the most troubled households. First the state is in laissez-faire mode, providing minimal or no therapeutic or personal support to parents. But if parents cross a line and abuse or neglect a child then the child is removed from the home. Later the parents might be put in jail and much later as the child grows that may be their destination as well. It is as if you have all the rights in the world until you have no rights. There needs to be a better balance of rights. And the rights of the child must come first.

Tolerating children and running public services the way we have up till now is not going to make Scotland the best place to bring up children. As you read on I trust you will come to see how we can unlock ourselves from the errors of the past.

It will take the next 10-20-30 years to change deep intergenerational patterns, but I am confident that we can shift attitudes, behaviour and priorities. Scotland can climb that telling UNICEF league table. We shall have to wait and see whether we could ever reach the top. Nonetheless, as I outline later, it is clear what first steps we need to take to get us on the way.

CHAPTER TWO
An epiphany

Given the importance of the first 1,000 days of life it is useful to reflect on what your own was like. Here's a snapshot of mine.

I was the product of a healthy pregnancy. I was born at home in a tenement in Bellshill, Lanarkshire. And I was breast-fed. As my mum did not normally smoke or drink alcohol, I can't imagine that she did so when pregnant. My father was no drinker either. Twice a year my dad would have a glass of alcoholic custard called Advocaat. My mum and dad were totally committed to each other. When I appeared, Peter my brother was ten years-old and my sister Irene at eight years-old became my second mum.

We moved to a council house when I was four. We had no car. Somewhere in my teenage years central heating appeared. Our parents made do, mended, lived within their means and, if driven to borrow, sought help from family members. My mother Jenny saved string, carefully removed wrapping paper to use again, collected buttons in boxes and had a formidable store of special-offer food cans. The values that ran through our house were about working hard, being considerate to others and not getting 'too big for your boots'.

There was no violence in the house other than a very occasional spank delivered by my father and my fights with my big brother. It's a tight race between what I liked least: the spanks or the brother. Fighting was part of life at primary school. Later in a Motherwell secondary school for clever boys I discovered a different scale of violence. For my first two years there I got two or three of the belt every day for getting my French vocabulary wrong. I detested the teacher and dreaded the class. But accepted it as normal.

My dad, a tool-maker, worked seven days a week in a very small engineering company he set up. As far back as I can remember my mum left the house every weekday to help out with the office work. My older sister cared for me, as did neighbours. Nearby lived my much-loved maternal grandmother. She was my mum number three. In my pre-school years I protested about being left with her during the working week. Now I wonder if I was left with others too much. Did I suffer from my parents not knowing enough about my small life? Or did they provide enough supportive scaffolding? This was the late 1950s and I always saw my mother and father in the middle of the day when they travelled to my gran's for a homemade lunch.

My home was not wealthy and I did not start out in life as middle class. Was I poor and didn't know it? Or was I rich and didn't know it? Like so many Scottish baby boomers born between 1946 and 1956, I suspect I was financially poor but rich in relationships. I was fortunate that there was no profound trauma in my early life. I was loved and looked after.

But this wasn't true of everyone. Of my four primary school pals two had parents who had separated and another regularly went hungry on Thursday, the night before payday. That means that three out of my four pals had at least one significant example of adversity in their early life. That is what we now term an Adverse Childhood Experience and multiple ACEs, as they are called, increase the likelihood of poor physical and mental health in later life. I explain more about this in Chapter Seven.

The lesson I draw from my childhood experience, and from reading and observation, is this: poverty is a problem, but it's what parents do and don't do that matters. It is not about how much money they have. Too little money is a problem and, so it seems, is too much money. There's a danger that we become too hung up on money. We see it as the determining factor of a good life.

Some of my peers made choices in life which had an unfortunate effect on their future. I have one striking memory of being at secondary school in Motherwell. I was sitting next to Jimmy Ryan, my best friend, but our paths were beginning to diverge. My mum liked having him in the house. He was smart. He was as charming as a 16 year-old can be. He played football for the school and basketball for Scotland. But Jimmy was like baby three in the maternity ward. In a fifth year English class Jimmy tapped my arm and told me that Janice, his girlfriend, was pregnant. The teacher shouted at us to stop talking. By then it was too late for the baby, Jimmy and Janice.

Evidently Jimmy had wanted sex. I do not know if Janice wanted a baby. I hardly knew her. But I did wonder if she took some of the alcohol and street drugs Jimmy was taking, and that was partly why she got pregnant. By sixth year Jimmy's trajectory meant he was not physically well enough to play basketball or football. I was at his funeral when he died in his early forties.

Scottish young people like Jimmy and Janice, aged 15 to 19, are five times more likely to have a child while still a teenager than their peers in Holland. There were 77,000 known pregnancies in Scotland that resulted in 54,000 live births in 2014-15. Roughly one in every six conceptions ends in termination. Out of the 54,000 live births, 2,270 were to teenage mothers. I am pained that one out of every 23 babies in Scotland is born to a teenager. This is much higher than neighbouring countries.

I asked the person running Scotland's largest single parent organisation why there were so many teenage mothers in Scotland. The answer was memorable: 'They are trying to get some love into their lives.' Once pregnant the choices and outcomes reduce. Abortion is not an easy option.

If significant harm occurs during any of these vital foundation stages then impairment will follow and show at school, in job prospects, in adult health and in relationships. These poor outcomes happen almost like night follows day. Some lucky people make it through relatively unscathed but that is against the odds.

A little bit wiser

I got a degree in economics and moral philosophy from St Andrews University and moved to my first job in Oxford working for Third World First, a campaigning organisation that emerged from Oxfam. Three years later I set up Scottish Education and Action for Development in Edinburgh to work on Scottish Third World connections. By this time I discovered that people who were on the side of the angels were good at talking and big on empathy. But were not good at organising. Later I squeezed in a Master of Business Administration degree from Edinburgh University.

In 1983 at the time of mass closure of traditional manufacturing, along with others I started a company called Heatwise Glasgow. Its aim was to draught-proof and insulate houses, provide temporary paid work to long-term unemployed people and help them get a job in the mainstream market. The company grew like Topsy, moved into environmental improvement, created urban forests, set up the first public glass recycling plant in Glasgow, ran a call centre and expanded into different parts of Scotland and England.

Over time the organisation became the Wise Group and I was the Chief Executive. We employed around 300 full-time people and each year helped over 2,000 previously long-term unemployed people into work. The Wise Group was acknowledged as one of the leading UK social enterprise companies. Visitors included Sir Peter Walker, Sir Tom Farmer, Tony Blair and Gordon Brown. They came to understand why we were so successful and to get a feel for our operations and business model. We were credited as being a role model for the New Deal and I added government advisory meetings in Westminster and Edinburgh to my schedule.

Our success in getting people employment in the mainstream job market came from two factors. Firstly, the people we recruited were down in the dumps. We gave them training and a job to do. Confidence and self respect grew, they mixed with different people, got into the discipline of work (well most) and received a pay packet. Secondly, from the outset we told them that the job was for one year; the responsibility of getting the next job in the open market was their responsibility. We systematically made help available to support their efforts. I would like you to remember this story when later I return to the subject of prevention and the goal of helping people to help themselves.

We developed a segmentation process to better understand the long-term unemployed people we recruited. They typically fell into one of three groups. It was easiest to find a job for the people who had worked for years but had stopped through bad luck like successive redundancies, illness or injury, or had taken a break to have children. There was also a middle group of people who were reasonably articulate and amiable and although not burning with enthusiasm, did try. They were in with a shout of getting a job.

There was a third group of people, mostly young men, who were depressed, agitated and angry. I remember sitting near our head of personnel when he leapt back from his desk as a young man pulled out a blade. Our front-line staff found it hard to engage with this group. They were not interested, did not talk much, stared a lot, were poor at turning up and took offence easily. Many were dressed in sports gear, had thin faces, pale complexions and homemade tattoos.

I discovered that our front-line staff had created their own designation; these were the 'starers'. Not a term I was that happy with but it did catch a truth. They were a long way from possessing the attributes that employers want. These young men and women often mumbled, 'I don't want a job', but that was a form of self-protection because they knew they were unemployable. They had in a sense left school many years before the official leaving date, were inarticulate and had few connections with people in work.

I doubt if the Wise Group, or anyone else, could retrofit

soft skills on to a 'starer'. The ramp we offered came too late and was insufficient. Their problems were deep and multiple. Employers want more than brawn.

There's another vital issue hiding here. Most of the 'starers' were already fathers. You could say that here was baby number four in our maternity ward, reproducing a new baby number four.

A golden moment

I used to joke with friends that the Wise Group was my baby. It was the cause of lost sleep, the pouring out of nurture and it caused endless worry. At the time I did not have children and I was not so sure (like 'starers' not wanting a job) that I wanted to go down this road. However, I became a late entrant to marriage at age 40. With a reasonable amount of hair and teeth intact, I became a first-time father at 47.

Our daughter Eva came first and, three years later, Thomas: so started the hardest job that I have ever unconditionally loved doing. Michele, my wife, was able to take off a year at each birth and I found that I wanted to spend time at home and not be at evening meetings and dinners. My brother Peter held a commonly held view. 'Babies only get really fun,' he told me, 'when they are about three years old and you can play and they react.' Not for me: sleep aside, I was instantly smitten.

If it had not been for this happy bash to the back of the head, I wonder if I would have stopped to hear the message that then came my way. Early years practitioners talk about a 'Golden Moment' when parents, usually mothers, become ultra-receptive to hearing what they should do and super-motivated to put it into practice. My Golden Moment was having children at the same time as trying to work out in my job at Scottish Enterprise how employers got the people they needed.

Six months before fatherhood I had moved to Scottish Enterprise to become Senior Director for Skills and Learning. The job had three parts: training which included Modern Apprenticeships and other youth and employment programmes, creating Careers Scotland and establishing Future Skills Scotland to provide labour market intelligence. In post-devolution Scotland this kind of information simply did not exist or was not robust.

Boldly stamped on the Scottish Enterprise tin was, 'Meeting the needs of employers by providing technical or vocational skills and meeting the needs of the emerging workforce'. There was just one problem. When Future Skills Scotland interviewed over 22,000 big and small employers in the public and private sector, the analysts found that the data told an unexpected story.

Employers who had recruited at least one new person in the previous year told us about the biggest problems they encountered with new employees. The new recruits were poor at talking and listening, working with one another and the public, and poor at elementary planning or problem solving. Employers of people in lower paid jobs, for example working in care or retail jobs, had the greatest dissatisfaction. Graduates, we were told, had the same soft skills shortage, just to a lesser extent.

This was, and is, a difficult message because successive governments and parents have invested in getting higher and higher skills. When I got a degree in the 70s, I was one out of ten in my age group. Today, one out of two young people go onto a degree programme. Employers were telling Future Skills Scotland that they had no problem finding people with higher skills. What they could not get enough of were people with the right attitude, character or soft skills.

The more you think about it, the more you realise that these soft skills are the basic attributes needed to manage life, and in particular being a parent, never mind getting a job. It was these soft or life skills that were missing in many of the people taken on by the Wise Group. It stands to reason that a hotel or coffee bar is more likely to take on a migrant worker who looks you in the eye and is pleasant and helpful, than a local with poor soft skills.

As these findings did not concur with orthodoxy, it made sense to road test them with employers, just in case we had gone off track. This was a decade ago and I still remember the vehemence of the response. The manager of a major salmon processing facility said: 'We pay more than the minimum wage and although there are lots of unemployed in our area we recruit most of our people from Portugal.' Another from southern Scotland told me: 'At least the Latvians come in when it snows.' The owner of a conservatory and double glazing company made it very clear that we were a lot of deaf eejits: 'I have been telling you for years that we can't get the right type of young people.'

I took the labour market results to the Scottish Enterprise Board and eyebrows were raised. They were perplexed and asked me to go away and find out how you got these soft, non-cognitive skills. I was also instructed to take the matter up with the Scottish Government.

Along with Stephen Boyle who headed up Future Skills, we

did a presentation to the most senior Scottish education civil servant and his team. After two hours of close questioning and discussion, the big chief of education closed the session by saying: 'Thank you that was most interesting. But it has nothing to do with us.'

As we left the room we murmured to one another, 'Did he really say that?' I would in retrospect re-scramble his words and conclude that the message was this: I have a phenomenal amount on my plate, what you are saying does not feature among my minister's interests so, although what you say may be true, thanks but no thanks. We stumble on the truth, dust ourselves off and continue blindly down the same faulty path.

I set in motion an exercise at Scottish Enterprise to find out how to learn the soft skills of talking and listening, working with one another and being able to solve problems. One night I attended an Allander Lecture in Edinburgh given by James Heckman. Originally a mathematician, Heckman gravitated to labour market economics, became a Chicago economics professor and won the Nobel Prize for the creation of a two-step statistical approach that offered a way to correct non-randomly selected samples.

In his presentation that night, Heckman laid it on the line that from the big data he analysed, the most significant gains in human capital and human development came very early in life, way before school. Heckman demonstrated that the rate of return from public investment in these vital early years was around 7-10% for higher risk families: a higher rate of return than from other types of state spend.

I smarted when he argued that employment training, or

insertion programmes as he called them, were in comparison a waste of time. Heavens, I had spent close on 20 years sweating down this particular mine. To my relief later, in response to my question he acknowledged that he did not know any studies that looked at the family or parenting consequences of helping young men and women find work.

By coincidence Carol Craig, the commissioning editor of this Postcards series, shared my journey home that night. I recall her asking me how I felt about Heckman's thesis. 'Perplexed' was my answer to Carol's question, 'I need more time to think about it'.

I have had that time. I burrowed into the literature, gave talks, wrote, '0-5: How Small Children Make a Big Difference', conversed with experts and received a Churchill Travelling Fellowship to spend time in Holland – where for good reason the children are judged to be the happiest in the world – and Finland, a high achiever in child well-being but a country like Scotland with a dark alcoholic inclination. I wanted to look under the carpet and find out what they did, did not do and what was important to them.

With new babies in my house I found myself stopping in the tracks that had been worn by a fast-moving life. What started as a quest to understand skills morphed into a more all-embracing quest and investigation. From 2008 until 2011, I acted as an unpaid Advisor to Noel Dolan, the paid Advisor to Nicola Sturgeon when she was the Health Secretary for Scotland. I knew Noel from many years back and what started as a lunch moved into a series of meetings showing why parenting and early years were a significant health issue. In turn I was asked to draw up a short list of practical measures with outline costs that could help to start tackling our endemic problem. The shortlist included more health visitors, the Family Nurse Partnership and Baby Boxes. More on these later.

I have met with heavyweight authorities in the UK, Holland, Finland and the USA, and also many 'ordinary' people whose stories resonated. Medical, biological, neuro-scientific, statistical, psychological and economic studies on pregnancy, birth and what parents do, are necessarily cautious. Each piece of research improves our understanding of the big picture by a degree or two. What works in that careful peer-reviewed academic world does not necessarily make sense to the rest of us trying to understand and improve our world.

One thing is now clear to me: both scientific research and practical on-the-ground work point unequivocally to one simple truth. In allowing generation after generation to experience damage in the womb and trauma and uncertainty in their first 1,000 days, we are condemning many of them to lives of poor quality with huge cost to society and the state.

I have in the following chapters picked out critical details from my research, point by point, to tell a story. It's a picture created through observation, reading, conversation, intimate confidences and a few wrong turns.

CHAPTER THREE

What science and research tells us about the early years

Having been knocked off my proverbial bicycle by Professor James Heckman's research, demonstrating that the best time to 'invest' in humans is before the age of three, I needed to find out more.

While on a business visit to Chicago I discovered that Heckman could not understand why the data produced the results that he got. On a visit to the Erikson Institute in Chicago, a renowned graduate school specialising in early years development, Dr Jana Fleming told me with a twinkle in her eye about the time she sat down with James Heckman to explain the ABCs of child development. Way before I met Jana, I turned to science to get some answers.

After some research I found three major studies, including a classic study cited by Heckman, which offered the depth of insight I sought. I also found more evidence of just how critical some aspects of Scotland's parenting problem have become.

Perry Preschool
In poor black inner city Michigan in the 1960s rampant school failure drove the director of special education to break from what they did before. This led to what is now known as the Perry Preschool Programme.

The foundations were practical: we know that children learn best through active experiences and following their own interests. Through play and making choices, they become naturally engaged. High quality nursery-cum-teaching staff were recruited and trained in child interaction, engaging in dialogue and how to help children reflect. This was on top of sessions on language, child conflict resolution, movement and music and creative representation.

Children were recruited at three years of age on the basis of being African-American, living in poverty and assessed to be at high risk of school failure. For the next two years they spent five half-days a week following the programme. This was supplemented by a weekly one and a half hour home visit.

A research methodology was put in place. A total of 123 children with an IQ lower than 90 were randomly assigned between a programme group that participated in the curriculum and home visits, and a control group that received no preschool programme. At the end of the two years both groups were followed up annually to the age of 11 and again at 14, 15, 19, 27 and 40 years.

Over time there was no recorded improvement in IQ. But 65% of the programme group finished high school against 45% of the control group. There was half the number of teenage births in the programme group and subsequently more births in wedlock.

Particularly significant were the research findings once the groups had reached the age of 40:

■ Prison: 28% of the programme group had been sent to prison compared to 52% of the control group

■ Employment: 76% of the programme group were in jobs against 52% of the control group

■ Earnings: median annual income was $5,000 more for the programme group.

■ Benefits: programme group members were 26% less likely to have used government assistance programmes.

■ Drugs: 17% of the male programme group used sedatives, sleeping pills or tranquillisers against 43% of the control group.

Given the selection process and random assignment between the control and programme group, the children's pre-school experience is the best explanation for the substantial differences in performance over the years.

The Perry Preschool study has three critical factors in common with other successful early interventions: an emphasis on quality, well-trained staff; a triangular programme design involving work with the child, work with the parent and work with the parent and child together; and finally a recognition that the scale of the support has to match the dimensions of the task at hand.

What the Perry Pre-School Programme shows is that as young as three there are distinctive 'markers' that predict that some children are likely to have miserable lives. But there is also a large dose of hope: a well thought-out and well-delivered intervention improved many of the programme group's lives for the better.

One study in 1960s inner city black America and its lessons are not immediately transferable to Scotland 50 years on. What worked for 58 children is not easily supersized to be made available to all of Scotland's 200,000 three and four year-olds. But the Perry Preschool approach could be made available to the three and four year-olds identified in Scotland as being open to abuse or neglect or not being 'looked after'.

Dunedin

I needed to examine the scientific evidence that the origins of our life-time big issues and trajectories already exist at the age of three.

The city of Dunedin, the Gaelic name for Edinburgh, is the capital of the Otago region in New Zealand. It has lots of Scots, sheep and the same kind of spread of income and wealth as Scotland. It is also home to arguably the most studied group of people in the world.

In 1972 the University of Otago embarked on a world-first study programme to observe the health and development of that year's new-borns over the decades of their lives. The Dunedin Multidisciplinary Health and Development programme is today still regarded as the global benchmark in assessing and measuring how people of all backgrounds develop in response to their environments.

In 1972 there were 1,039 babies born in the greater Otago region. Three years later 1,037 of the children with their parents' agreement were observed, assessed and measured as part of a multidisciplinary exercise. The children covered the full socio-economic range. Every two years up to the age of 11 they were assessed and measured and again at 15, 18, 21, 26, 32 and 38 years.

After four decades 961 of the original group (93%) are still in the study. About a quarter now live outside New Zealand but the participants are committed and the research team is diligent. Usually in studies it is the wayward that fall out – the homeless, peripatetic and those generally cut off from society, and their absence throws the results off kilter. Not here: this is a statistically significant group of people that has been studied over time in breadth and depth.

Breadth takes in mental health including substance abuse, intimate relationships including domestic violence, oral health, sexual and reproductive health, respiratory health, retinal imaging and cardiovascular risk. Information is gathered on employment, personality, anti-social behaviour and criminality, childhood adversity, cognition and neuro-psychology.

Depth means carrying out cardiovascular tests, dental examinations, blood tests and more. Crosschecking takes place for veracity: for example you might report that you only drink moderately, less than 21 units a week (the UK and Scottish recommended limit is now 14 units a week) – but what do people say who know you? Similarly with hard drugs and criminality, the researchers have permission to go beyond what participants report.

Over 40 years of accumulating such rich data has enabled a virtual industry of academic miners to produce over a thousand studies. For example the study and its data have contributed to an understanding of the effects of long-term cannabis use at midlife.

The most significant finding from the team of international researchers over these four decades is the following:

> 'Self-control in childhood is more important than
> socio-economic status or IQ in predicting adults'
> physical health, wealth, life satisfaction, addiction,
> crime, and the parenting of the next generation.'

The message is again clear. The most precious, determining part of life happens very early.

At age three and then again at 5, 7, 9 and 11 years the Dunedin researchers had four different sources of information:

- observations on what the children were doing including a formal assessment of traits and abilities

- parent reports

- reports from nursery staff and teachers

- self-reporting from the children.

What the researchers found at three years of age was largely confirmed in the years that followed. Children exhibited a range of 'self-control' skills or attributes: at the poor end these involved being unable to wait for a turn, fleeting attention, impulsive, low frustration tolerance, requiring constant attention and motivation from an adult, going for risky options, disliking putting effort into a task and lacking persistence.

In adulthood these characteristics are displayed in such behaviours as speaking before you think, saying what hurts or is inappropriate, acting out, jumping to conclusions, not resisting temptations and pre-emptive tit-for-tat – hurt someone before they hurt you. Not unlike my Glasgow starers.

At ages 32 and 38, it was the adults with the best mental and physical health who had previously displayed the greatest self-control at ages three and five. The children who had the worst self-control at three and five years had the worst health as adults.

Substance abuse was worst for the children with poor self-control. The best protection from abuse of alcohol and drugs was found to be childhood self-control.

Adults who financially struggled and saved least for retirement had the lowest self-control as children, while those successfully managing their finances and building a pension had the best performance when very young. Participants with the highest incidence of criminal conviction had the lowest self-control at three and five years.

But. . . are these children with high self-control also buttoned-up automatons? On the contrary: the evidence suggests that they have the best mental health and report the greatest happiness and satisfaction. Friends and family also rate them as the most satisfied.

Across the spectrum of health, substance abuse, personal finances, criminal behaviour and life satisfaction, there is a direct connection between the degree of self-control achieved at childhood and what happens as adults. Willpower, the ability to stop and think through consequences, regulate emotions, weigh up a situation – these represent a package of self-controlling attributes that protects their owners from the downsides of life. Even better, these competences guide them to get the best out of their circumstances. The Dunedin study found that at ages three and five it was already apparent that the participant children covered a range exhibiting high, medium and low self-control. How children are likely to attain self-control will emerge later.

Prediction, prevention and early intervention
Using the data from the Dunedin study Professor Avshalom Caspi (Duke University and King's College London) and a group of

other academics have advanced our understanding of prediction and how in turn that can assist prevention. By combining administrative data for each individual in the longitudinal study they aggregated different types of economic burden. They applied a segmentation approach along the lines of the Pareto 80:20 maxim, that is, 80% of the effects are found in just 20% of the people studied.

What they found at age 38 was that 22% of the children/adults were responsible for the following outcomes and costs:

81% of criminal convictions

78% of prescriptions

77% of fatherless child rearing

66% of welfare benefits

57% of hospital nights

54% of cigarettes smoked

40% of excess kilograms

36% of injury insurance claims.

Four predictors were found for these outcomes: socio-economic deprivation, IQ, maltreatment and poor self-control/brain health.

One predictor in particular stood out: 'brain health' gauged through a small bank of tests that take 45 minutes to administer at age three. The test predicted with accuracy 80% of the time. It involved a neurological examination and assessments of verbal comprehension, language development, motor skills, and social behaviour.

To summarise: the heaviest burden of outcomes from criminal conviction to hospital nights and being over-weight were concentrated on 22% of the 1,000 Dunedin participants.

What happens before three years of age that produces these results? What are the public policy implications, given that as we have seen, before early intervention comes prevention, and before prevention comes prediction? In today's public sector, spend is focused on symptoms and you can only administer a new intervention if it results in a saving to your budget – not a gain to the wider community or public purse.

Looking at this from the perspective of the person with the burden, they face multiple pains. They are people who are anxious, stressed, go more often to their GP and A&E, have some addiction issues, have psychological needs, self-harm (more likely if a woman), get operated on for swallowing batteries and have the police looking for them as a 'missing person'. All this is before turning to look at what this litany does to their children.

A heavy burden: looked-after children in Scotland

The Audit Commission in Scotland in its most recent examination of looked-after children shows that in 2008/9 there were 1,600 young Scottish people in residential care at an average cost of £156,250 per annum: a total public cost that year of £250 million. If costs have risen in line with inflation the bill in 2017 will be around £310 million.

In 2016/17 in my home city of Glasgow 239 children were in residential care at an average annual cost of £176,000. This amounts to a total cost of £42 million a year to look after 239 children. Even more starkly within that group of 239 children, there were 93 children, most of whom found foster care too difficult to manage and were placed in specialist residential care at an average cost of £228,000 a year. Gross average annual income in Scotland in 2016 was £22,900.

The scale of this spend is so large that it takes up 44% of the Children and Families budget in Glasgow and leaves little scope for preventative or therapeutic work for the even larger group of 'drowning' parents and children.

I fear that the £310 million plus a year spent in Scotland on looked-after children is more about containment than investment. Much of this failure in parenting could have been predicted and the consequences mitigated if not avoided. We know from the Dunedin study that the personal and social cost does not stop here: 22% of the most damaged adults at 38 years of age created by far the biggest burden on the public purse.

A recent sample of 250 childcare cases in Glasgow confirmed that nearly 51% of the children and young people were known to social services at birth. The parents had themselves been in care or were known alcohol and drug abusers. Engagement with the families is often hostile, frequently fraught and always a challenge.

In the face of significant financial pressure and no shortage of families needing help Glasgow Children Services deserve applause for redirecting their work. Based around the principles of helping more families to help themselves and directing resources to early help, they are changing how they work. An audit of family support services revealed: 'Prevention infra-structure is weak, haphazard and inadequate.' A new aim has emerged to reclaim the front line of social work and to get in earlier to help and support families. This will involve re-skilling social workers, tying in more with alcohol and drug workers, working more with health visitors, substantially increasing cooperation with voluntary organisations experienced at working with families and children and wherever possible providing kinship care rather than institutional care for children removed from the parental home.

With a reduction of just six in the number of highest-cost children and 26 in the next most expensive group – with alternatives being found – the potential annual saving comes to £7.4 million. Making this change allows funds to be redirected up-stream to health visitors and voluntary organisations to prevent problems arising. It is a good start.

Three-year-olds in Scotland
Edinburgh is the home of a Scottish national study, Growing Up in Scotland (GUS). Children born between June 2004 and May 2005 were selected at random from the Child Benefit register. The parents gave their agreement to participate. Interview data was collected once a year from the age of ten months to six years of age.

In 2011 researchers drew from a body of evidence covering 3,600 children and their families and produced the paper, 'Changes in Child Cognitive Ability in the Pre-School Years'. At the ages of three and five years the researchers dug in to find the children's problem-solving competence and ability with vocabulary. The differences in ability are largely expressed in standard deviations and if you are statistically inclined the references are given at the end. A more straightforward under-standing comes through reporting the difference in average scores as an 'age equivalent'. This is based on the progress that would be expected of a typical child at the relevant age.

The research team only calculated the 'age-equivalent' at five years of age and not at three years. But the differences between the two sets of results are so minor, I will quote the results as a combined three-five year range.

Problem solving is an attribute needed for life and, as you may remember, one of employers' most highly valued skills. Children born to parents with no qualifications were at three years of age ten months behind the average child in the Growing Up in Scotland group – and a staggering 13 months behind the children born to parents with a degree.

When it came to language, the researchers showed that children at three and five years of age whose parents had a degree possessed a vocabulary 18 months ahead of children whose parents had no qualifications.

If this were a three year-olds' sports day in the race for life, we as spectators would watch a large bunch of children hobbling along with both legs tied together before tumbling over. Many others would be ambling along at reasonable speeds. Another group will have finished and be out of sight.

A similar story is told in another GUS study, 'Growing Up in Scotland: Health Inequalities in Early Years'. From three years and before, the odds stack up against some children: they have more experience of long-term health problems and more accidents. And these small children are more exposed to risk factors that last a lifetime: their mother's health is poor, there is less physical activity, more smoking in the house and poor diet from a combination of reduced breastfeeding, more sugary drinks and less fresh vegetables.

Are our children doomed?

From Detroit to Dunedin and back to Scotland via Glasgow, it becomes abundantly clear that at the age of three, many children have already been marked for life.

This major finding opens up two profound questions. First – is this fatalism? Are we destined (doomed?) to follow the imprint that already exists at three years of age?

No, this is not about day following night, it is about likelihood and risk. What has been identified is a major factor influencing children's futures – brain health and self-control. But this discovery also offers the possibility of actions to reduce the risk of a poor future for that child. At three years the child's brain and behaviour is more malleable than at 17. Early intervention from parents, nursery staff and health workers can make a difference.

The second question flows from the first: what can be done to make sure – or as sure as we can – that by the time this little soul leaves the maternity ward and grows to a three year-old that they have self-control? How can their life chances be enhanced to give them an opportunity to flourish? Or, in the language of health and public policy: what can be done to prevent physical, emotional and mental harm?

What steps need to be taken by parents, society and public services to make sure that future generations of three year-olds are not sent on a life course with one arm tied behind their back and a hobbled leg?

The rest of the book opens out, and answers as best I can, this vital question.

Recovery

To illustrate the potential that young children have for recovery from a poor start in life, let's look at a case study from the US child psychiatrist Bruce Perry, the Senior Fellow of the Child Trauma Academy in Houston, Texas.

Justin's mother was a 15 year-old girl who left him with her own mother when he was two months old. Justin's grandmother was a kind-hearted and nurturing woman who adored her grandchild. Unfortunately she was also morbidly obese and with related health problems died when Justin was around twelve months old.

Arthur, a passive man in his late sixties, the live-in partner of the grandmother, baby-sat for Justin. Help did not come from social services, he was out of his depth and ignorant about the caring needs of children and did what he knew best. He made a living as a dog breeder and applied that knowledge to Justin. He began to keep Justin in a dog cage. He made sure he was changed and fed but rarely spoke or played with him.

For five years Justin largely lived in the cage with dogs as his primary companions. When Bruce Perry met Justin now aged six in a Paediatric Intensive Care Unit, he was shrieking, bony and wore a loose diaper. He rocked back and forth, whimpered a self-soothing lullaby and was filthy with his own faeces and had food over his face.

It turned out that Arthur had over the years taken Justin to the doctors to see why Justin had poor motor skills, behavioural issues and not made sufficient cognitive and language progress. After brain scans and chromosomal analysis the message came back from different doctors that Justin had 'static encephalopathy' – most likely due to some unknown and untreatable birth defect. American medical and social care systems are even more fragmented than in Scotland and no one had followed his case over time or gone behind the curtain to find out what really happened at home, or in this case the cage. Arthur was not insensitively cruel – he did take Justin and the dogs out of their cages daily for play and affection. But the boy was denied virtually every opportunity to develop normally.

Perry carefully got Justin to relate to him and built up trust. He was the first person to be told by Arthur about his child-rearing practices, because he was the first person to ask. In therapy he tried to imagine the world from Justin's perspective. Along with Perry's intervention came physical and language therapists, as well as language and occupational therapy for fine motor skills. Justin responded to the new repetitive patterns of stimulation.

After two weeks Justin was transferred to a nearby foster family, with continuing support. Six months later Justin moved to a foster family who lived much further away. About two years later a note came from the family. Justin was doing well, rapidly hitting development milestones that no one ever expected him to reach. Now at eight there was a picture of Justin holding a lunch box, wearing a backpack and standing next to the school bus.

'This was the most rapid recovery from severe neglect that we had seen,' wrote Perry. 'It changed my perspective on the potential for change following early neglect'.

What are the lessons from this story? Hope over fatalism – marked improvements can be made to damaged lives by simple steps. And it helps if the period in the womb is healthy and that the serve and return between the baby and caregiver lays down the best foundation for brain and biological development.

CHAPTER FOUR

In Scotland we tolerate children

Eva Kocovska was born in Prague, Czechoslovakia when the country was a Soviet satellite, got her doctorate in pharmaceutical research before moving to Sweden where she had her first baby. A few years later her second child was born in Leicester – and the family decamped to Glasgow and raised their two girls.

Eva remembers her mum being treated as a pariah in Czechoslovakia. She had opted to stay at home and rear her children. This was way out of line with the prevailing institutional Soviet orthodoxy: there were state nurseries that knew how to look after children and the woman's place was at work.

Sweden was different. Eva became familiar with some of the mums-to-be when along with her husband she made trips to the hospital during pregnancy. She discovered the birthing chair: common in Sweden but new to her, and opted to put it to use when the time came. For five days she stayed in a shared room with three other new mothers, at the Royal Hospital of Uppsala. It was a brilliant time, she recalls and so helpful.

Everyone who came into her room from the doctor to the cleaner could see that Eva struggled to speak Swedish so they talked in English. At night around 10pm, very quietly the nurses would take the babies to a separate room making it easier for the mothers to get a good sleep. Discretely during the small hours of the night babies would be returned to the mothers for breastfeeding. During the day gentle guidance and instruction was there on diet for mother and breastfeeding for the child, how to cope with and manage crying – even protracted crying – and what to look out for in the weeks ahead. Twenty-odd years later Eva recalls how tasteful her room was in the hospital and the appetising table with food and fresh fruit juice.

Eva and her husband both had PhDs, but back at their apartment in Uppsala they were struggling with no family support, a new language, long dark days and a shortage of money. Eva's family had sent three sets of clothes for baby Elizabeth, her only clothes.

One day, Eva remembers, Elizabeth had just soiled her clothes. Her other two sets were newly washed and still wet. At any moment the health visitor was due. What would she make of Eva as a migrant and mother, would she think she was hopeless and could not take care of a child?

'Do not worry,' said the health visitor; 'no matter, put the bib on to protect her skin and when her clothes are dry put them on'. Immediately Eva relaxed, felt at ease and began to realise that if she was not anxious, there was a good chance that baby Elizabeth would be fine. Not long after, thanks to the health visitor, Eva was connected to a 'parish group' made up of other new mothers in the neighbourhood.

Jobs changed and Eva, her husband and Elizabeth moved to Leicester and in quick succession baby number two followed. 'My maternity hospital was awful,' said Eva, 'it was worse than Prague. There were ten of us in a room and no one slept. There was no personal involvement of the staff; they seemed to have neither the time nor the capacity to help. And the food was dreadful and we only had tea to drink.' And when you left hospital you quickly said good-bye to your health visitor and that was that – you were on your own.

'Why do you,' Eva asked me, 'bring up your babies in the Soviet way?'

The league of child well-being

I took Eva to task for stopping at two children. As part of a scientific husband and wife team, I thought she should have a peripatetic life and have a child in a new country every fifteen months for the next 15 years and provide a baby travelogue! A Lonely Planet for parents and babies. Funnily enough, she did not think it was such a good idea.

The United Nations International Children's Emergency Fund (UNICEF), through its Innocenti Research Centre, produced a report in 2013 titled 'Child Well-Being in 29 of the World's Advanced Economies'. In this work the analysts compared 26 internationally used indicators on children spread across five categories:

- Material well-being including monetary and material deprivation and levels of inequality.

- Health and safety including birth weight and rates of immunisation.

- Education including measures of early childhood education and the number of 15-19 year-olds not in employment, training or education, as well as average PISA (maths, language and science) scores.

- Behaviours and risk with attention given to weight,

teenage fertility, rate of use of alcohol and cannabis and measures on fighting and bullying.

- ■ Housing and environment.

These measures include risky pre-birth behaviours of parents and continue up to the late teenage years, giving us a picture of the flow of childhood experience for each country and allowing us to benchmark how we are doing.

Composite measures such as this provide a reliable window (much more reliable than flogging one statistic or anecdote) on parenthood and childhood. If as a very small person we had the choice, it would tell us which country would be best for our prospects. A league table of the statistics available in 2013 is set out oppposite.

At the top of the table comes the Netherlands, followed by Norway, Iceland and Finland. At the bottom come three of the poorest countries, all ex-Soviet and satellite states – Latvia, Lithuania and Romania. Just above the bottom three countries languishes one of the richest and most unequal, the United States.

In 16th place is the United Kingdom, a reasonable proxy for Scotland. Eva's comparison of the UK and Scotland as adopting the Soviet approach to parenting, originally seemed to me to be outlandish. Yet in the table the Czech Republic, her and her mother's native place, scores marginally better than the UK. It is hard to admit but the data supports Eva's observation. Parenting and child well-being in Scotland are close to Eva's Soviet satellite experience.

On taking up her post in November 2017 Maree Todd, the Minister for Early Years and Childcare in Scotland, repeated the

	Overall well-being	Dimension 1	Dimension 2	Dimension 3	Dimension 4	Dimension 5
	Average rank all 5 dimensions	Material well-being	Health and safety	Education	Behaviours and risks	Housing and envoronment
		[rank]	[rank]	[rank]	[rank]	[rank]
1 Netherlands	2.4	1	5	1	1	4
2 Norway	4.6	3	7	6	4	3
3 Iceland	5	4	1	10	3	7
4 Finland	5.4	2	3	4	12	5
5 Sweden	6.2	5	2	11	5	8
6 Germany	9	11	12	3	6	13
7 Luxembourg	9.2	6	4	22	9	5
8 Switzerland	9.6	9	11	16	11	1
9 Belgium	11.2	13	13	2	14	14
10 Ireland	11.6	17	15	17	7	2
11 Denmark	11.8	12	23	7	2	15
12 Slovenia	12	8	6	5	21	20
13 France	12.8	10	10	15	13	16
14 Czech Rep	15.2	16	8	12	22	18
15 Portugal	15.6	21	14	18	8	17
16 UK	15.8	14	16	24	15	10
17 Canada	16.6	16	27	14	16	11
18 Austria	17	7	26	23	17	12
19 Spain	17.6	24	9	28	20	9
20 Hungary	18.4	18	20	8	24	22
21 Poland	18.8	22	18	9	19	26
22 Italy	19.2	23	17	25	10	21
23 Estonia	20.8	19	22	13	26	24
23 Slovakia	20.8	25	21	21	18	19
25 Greece	23.4	20	19	28	25	25
26 USA	24.8	26	25	27	23	23
27 Lithuania	25.2	27	24	19	29	27
28 Latvia	26.4	28	28	20	28	28
29 Romania	28.6	29	29	29	27	29

Table 1: League table of child well-being

29 developed countries are ranked based on the average of five factors

general ambition of the Scottish Government: 'We want Scotland to be the best place in the world to grow up.' This may be a tall order.

Take a look at this table as though it were the Scottish

Football League at the end of the 2016-17 season. Celtic would be at the top in the place of the Netherlands. Inverness Caledonian Thistle in the twelfth relegation slot i.e. above the UK's league position in the UNICEF table. Can you imagine being the manager of Caley Thistle and told by your directors to (choose your cliché) get your finger out, pull your socks up and knock Celtic off their perch? You would be advised to find another club before getting the elbow.

It is good to have an aspiration but if it is to become a serious intent, actions need to match words. In our football analogy, if it were to come to pass, there would have to be dramatic financial and managerial improvements, and a major investment in creating a better-trained, skilful and motivated team.

In the real world our collective aspiration would need to change, political decision-making would need to re-orientate, health services re-calibrate and above all our personal and communal parenting approach would need to up its game. More on this later.

Does the UNICEF test made earlier this decade hold good today for Scotland? I have with friends and colleagues looked into some of the more recent Scottish figures. There has been a reduction in teenage use of alcohol at 15 years of age. A number of measures remain more or less the same, immunisation and birth weight. The proportion of children living in poverty has increased from 17% of households to 19%. And Scotland's (PISA) performance in school-age reading and science has in comparison to other nations dropped between 2012 and 2015. Some equivalents could not be found on housing and bullying. A more recent report from UNICEF in the Report Card series has switched the focus away from child well-being to meeting the UN development goals, so sticking with the 2013 table is our current best guide to well-being.

Of course statistics can be seen but not heard. In one UNICEF study into childrearing practices in the UK, Spain and Sweden researchers interviewed children individually and in groups. The researchers had permission to film families going about their daily business at home: a type of real-life Gogglebox with the results played back and analysed by national panels. There are limits to national generalisations – but they tell us something and we all do it.

In each country children spontaneously mentioned the same three factors that made them happy – or made a good day:

- spending time with those they love – friends, family and pets

- being creative or taking part in sporting activities

- having fun and being outdoors.

On the other side a bad day for children in all three countries came from arguments and disruption to family life and fights with parents and siblings.

In Sweden there was an emphasis on children helping out, sharing tasks like laying the table, cooking and gardening. Childhood is seen as a time of preparation for becoming a responsible adult.

British parents tied to long work hours and commuting found it harder to spend time with their children. British parents said that they felt tremendous pressure to purchase material goods for their children. This compulsive consumption was almost completely absent in Sweden and Spain.

In all three countries children did not see material possessions as essential to their well-being – with the exception of poor children in the UK. For some parents gadgets and clothes made up for lack of time. Poorer parents and children saw goods and brands as a way of protecting children from bullying and a way of holding on to respect.

This all rings true: in the majority of Scottish households both parents have jobs, although we can't forget that in one out of six households no-one goes to work. Respect, keeping face, making up for guilt and not letting the kids down is translated into game consoles and flash toys. Apparently some people believe or at least behave as if objects can replace time and effort and cloak guilt.

I decided to look at the best and learn. With the help of the Winston Churchill Memorial Trust I visited two countries at the top of the table: the Netherlands, with an economy and political system much like Scotland's, and Finland, a high scorer but like us a country of dark winter nights, with a formidable thirst for alcohol and a predisposition towards heart attacks.

Going Dutch

During pregnancy at week 34 Dutch mums have a visit from the Kraamzorg, a qualified healthcare professional, to discuss the type of support she needs for a home or hospital birth: 90% of births in Holland take place in the home, it is the norm. A Kraamzorg is paid through the comprehensive health insurance service. After the birth for typically eight days and up to eight hours a day the Kraamzorg comes to the house to aid the mum's recovery, make sure that the home and baby are clean, assist with feeding and have a keen eye on the baby's development. They even do the shopping and some cooking, so that mum can totally focus on the new person in their midst. Extra Kraamzorg support is available if there are already a number of children in the house, the home is 'unstable' or there are problems with feeding the baby. Dutch new mothers consider the Kraamzorg as a gift from God.

As the Kraamzorg helper moves out the Consultatiebureau – Mother and Baby Well-Being Clinics – slides in. The Clinics are the centrepiece of support from birth to school age, and have been a keystone of preventative health and early intervention for over 100 years in Holland.

One home visit is made shortly after birth. Then the parent(s) and baby visit the clinic in weeks 4 and 8, then in months 3, 4, 6, 7, 9, 11, 14 and 18, with further visits at years 2, 3 and finally 3 years and 9 months. Doctors at the clinic attend to general health, social and emotional development, motor skills and language development, while the nurses concentrate on baby care, parenting, feeding, toileting and sleeping. Back-up for health and development is provided by walk-in surgeries and a telephone helpline.

Although provided by the state this is a human and very personal service. But 'service' does not seem the right word as it suggests an efficient industrial-type process. Instead what you see is a set of relationships, first names and a familiarity with your back-story, all built through continuity of contact with the same nurse and doctor. It is truly comprehensive and welcome whether on the seventh floor of a tower block or in the home of an international management consultant.

In Victorian Scotland the provision of clean water and sewerage systems brought wholesale health benefits across the entire population. In Holland at the same time the public health community moved on from water and sanitation to confront the next big challenge: better parenting. In Scotland we have still to make that move while in Holland they are ramping up still further – or more appropriately, introducing a new generation of hugs for parents.

Gerda

In a Family Centre attached to a Mother and Baby Well-Being Clinic in Laak, a high rise, low-income area in The Hague, nurse Gerda told me a story about supporting a mother of three boys. Two of them had learning difficulties and two were diabetic; the father was violent. On top of depression and isolation the family had enormous debts.

Family Centres have a working principle of 'one family, one plan'.

When she started Gerda counted eight different services and professionals visiting the family. Over a number of weeks after getting to know the mother and the boys, Gerda made the judgement that there was something in the mother that could be built upon. During the week the boys were put into care, coming home at weekends, while Gerda and the mother talked and worked through exercises on self-control, dealing with depression, parenting, debts and isolation. A year later the boys were going to come back home – but no, the mother was not ready and a second year was put in place. The violent dad died.

At the end of two years, the boys returned home for longer periods before moving back to the house permanently. A course of action was worked out for the boys to do more for themselves. A schedule was agreed for Gerda to withdraw but still be available in case the mother got stuck. Three years after the initial contact was made the mother told Gerda, 'I feel I can do it'. All was not perfect, how could it be? But close on twelve months after Gerda withdrew, the mother was coping, the house and family were functioning and the oldest boy had settled into mainstream school.

In Scotland the family would be monitored to see if the children were badly neglected and being abused. Personal and therapeutic support might or might not be available. If it were really, really bad the children would be removed. In Holland the mum has been helped to cope. In Scotland it is the blind eye. The steady drip of personal pain and social costs, the burden, last a lifetime.

People who are very good at something are not complacent; they know that they could be even better. In the years before my visit a range of teenage problems were very visible to the authorities but they knew that the cause of these problems came early in life. No one owned the problem; there was a lack of cooperation between different services; there was insufficient help for parents and children. Support needed to be timely and tailored.

Central government shared the view and acted because, for too many young children, what was happening in their lives was not as it should be. I visited Professor Guus Schrijvers, of the public health department in the medical faculty of Utrecht University. He told me how he was one of the three people called in to advise the government on what to do in the face of rising levels of Attention Deficit Hyperactivity Disorder (ADHD), autism and stress-related disorders in children, not to mention violence on the streets and suicide. Schrijvers argued that parents were psycho-pathologising their children's behaviour and, at root, 'parents do not know how to handle their children'.

Out of this shared concern between local and central government, Holland – already at the top of the table of child well-being – is rolling out a plan to set up Family Centres, like the one Gerda works in, across every neighbourhood, in all 418 municipalities. The Family Centres complement the Mother and Baby Well-Being Clinics. They anticipate or spot problems, give guidance and counselling and coordinate local care. Mother and Baby Well-Being Clinics and now Family Centres are part of the lives of all Dutch mothers, fathers and young children.

During my visit I dropped in to the Amsterdam Science Museum. Looking over my shoulder I found my children Eva and Thomas having a French kiss courtesy of two large pinkish tongued glove puppets. Nearby were models explaining reproduction and a kit for making bubbles. Discussion and sheer openness about sex and sex education certainly play a part in the maturity that defines family relationships across Holland. But there is more.

In Scotland there are five times as many teenage mothers as in Holland. This gives an indication of how together a country is, and what problems lie in store. Teenage abortion rates are also substantially higher in Scotland. In general here it is the more vulnerable and needy teenagers who have babies.

'Even our lower layer of society want a chance and do not want a baby,' a Dutch Government policy advisor told me. 'And there are a lot of chances in the Netherlands'. Young people wanted to feel some control over their lives.

In Scotland and the UK it has become fashionable in political circles to see child day care as the route to a good start in life. In the Netherlands formal day care is patchy, parents moan, it is hard to find and generally thought to be inadequate. What mothers and fathers of young children do is take time off by working a percentage of the week and spending more time at home. Grandparents on bicycles, in trains and in cars make up the difference. On its own, day care in Holland does not contribute to its child well-being pole position.

'Happiest kids in the world'

Rina Accosta was brought up in the San Francisco Bay area by immigrant Philippino parents who sacrificed themselves (and repeatedly told her so) in order to give her a good education and a better life. Her parents managed their incomes to send Rina to a private Catholic girls school. She was on the way to becoming a doctor and doing medical research when she met a Dutch man doing post-graduate work. She married the love of her life, moved to Holland, had two children and ten years later co-authored a book with Michele Hutchison, *The Happiest Kids in the world: Bringing up children the Dutch way*.

Michele Hutchison grew up in England and describes her childhood as one big competition. Her parents moved house so that she could get into a good grammar school, getting the right grades were the fast track to a successful life. Her weekends were spent touring the country competing in swimming events. She was an ambitious young workaholic pursuing a career in publishing when she met a Dutch man, moved to Holland, had two children – and met Rina.

'Being a parent in the Netherlands has changed the way Rina and I are bringing up our children,' writes Michele. 'It has had an effect on our attitudes and how we think and feel about parenting. It has also altered how we behave.'

With the benefit of their Dutch perspective, what these mothers have come to see is that in the UK and USA the human drive to want the best for children has morphed into a hungry desire: wanting our children to be the best. In their native countries they see a 'pervasive alarmism' and anxiety among their peers – desperate for their children to succeed and be better than other children. Peers in the UK and the USA with young children just do not have enough time, are harassed and guilt-ridden.

Rina and Michele now recognise how they imported this baggage into their lives in Holland. Like cartoon characters running flat out till their heels dig into the dirt and great plumes of dust are sent into the air, the authors moved from reluctant participants to advocates for a more relaxed, simpler approach to childhood and family life.

During Rina's first pregnancy a neighbour explained that pregnancy and labour were normal events and not a medical condition. It was 'gezellig' (cosy and warm) to have children at home: she had her children in the very room where they were having a cup of tea. As soon as they had their children (in hospital or at home) in stepped the Kraamzorg to help with breast-feeding, nappy-changing, giving tea and biscuits to visitors and, if there were any, attending to the older children. For new mothers it reduced anxiety. For others the Kraamzorg's knowledge of how to screen for depression plays a vital role in keeping home life on the tracks at a stressful time.

'Giving birth the Dutch way does seem to create the best,

most supportive environment for new mothers,' say Rina and Michele. The authors know that if they had stayed in their native countries they would have been on their own with their new babies.

The Dutch take the work-life balance very seriously. People leave work early for the day if they have child commitments – no questions asked. One in four men, across both professional and manual trades, and three out of four women work part-time in the Netherlands. More men and women make the choice to work part-time. That compares to about one in five working part-time in other developed countries. Both Rina and Michele report that their partners and other fathers in Holland have a more equal role in child rearing.

At first Michele scoffed when the Mother and Baby Well-Being Clinic gave her the blue book, a 'Growth Guide'. At its core are the three Rs: Rust, Regelmaat en Reinheid – Rest, Regularity and Cleanliness. But it dawned on Michele that Dutch parents do not complain of sleep deprivation. A study has shown that on average Dutch babies get two hours of extra sleep a day than equivalent American babies – that passes on as two hours extra sleep or relaxation for parents.

Both mothers were 'mothered' by friends and family, the Kraamzorg and the Mother and Baby Well-Being Clinic. They were able to relax and keep calm; knowing that doing their best is good enough. They followed the mantra that babies respond to a regular daily routine.

Put the baby to bed when it is tired and before it falls asleep. Be calm, make sure the baby is fed and has a clean nappy, reduce outside distraction and practise the 'cry-out' method. If on retreating from the room the baby falls asleep – job done. If the baby cries out, wait perhaps one minute, maybe five, ten at the most then go back into the room, talk soothingly to the baby, but do not pick the baby up. Continue to do this till the baby falls asleep.

For Michele with the help of crying out and reassurance her first baby slept for a continuous eight hours after moving to solids around six months of age. The second child slept through from six weeks to six months and, as though to prove that every child is different, had more problems falling asleep when she moved to solids, partly on account of reflux. Albeit reluctantly she conceded that there was something in the method and coaching. If she could be more relaxed as a mother then the baby would be more relaxed.

This practice known as 'sleep training' is not consistently supported by research on experience. Others advocate that with exclusively breastfed babies it is evolutionary and normal for human babies and other primates to sleep in bed with the parents in the first months and be automatically breastfed every two or three hours.

As the children grew they joined 'play groups' where the emphasis was on unstructured play, not numbers, shapes or the alphabet. Irma, the play group teacher, explained that the aim was to socialise through playing with each other, sharing, being patient and feeling confident in group activities. For Irma it was not about 'monkeys' performing tricks with numbers or letters – it was about fully developing a person's learning to speak their minds and get along with other children. A soft skills message in tune with what employers told Scottish Enterprise and the self-control finding in Dunedin.

As the children grow they play outside unsupervised and out of sight of the parents. Parents balance involvement with their offspring with benign neglect. Simplicity runs through birthday parties that stick to a soft drink, a song and a biscuit, or the norm of passing on and receiving second-hand toys. In school the first years are about play, behaviour and relationships with teachers and other children.

Both Rina and Michele have had to wrestle with the culture they inherited from their own parents in moving from a set of values about academic, sporting and musical achievement to one based on contentment and life satisfaction. As the Dutch saying goes, 'What the old cock crows, the young cock learns'.

Holland is comparatively rich and equitable, parents spend time with their young babies, children play in the street, teenage parenthood is rare and there is a good preventative health system linked to excellent social services directed at parents and young children. Underlying this is a sentiment quoted earlier by a woman I know who spent the first half of her life in Holland and the second half in Scotland.

I asked for her opinion on raising children in the two countries. 'In Scotland you tolerate children,' she told me 'In the Netherlands we love children'.

The Finnish way

Across Finland there are Well Baby Clinics that do the same job as the Mother and Baby Well-Being Clinics in Holland. Ingrid, a young mother, paused as we entered a clinic in Espo, the home of Nokia. She translated the sign on the door: 'If your baby is sick do not come in here.' This is a health centre dedicated to prevention, early intervention and the functioning of the family unit. Kicking off my snow-covered shoes and padding about in my socks I met Tua, the nurse who had been such a constant in the life of Ingrid and her two children that she was now considered a friend.

With her first child Ingrid found the coaching and support invaluable. By the time of her second child, being a more confident mother she skipped some of the planned visits. If the Well Baby Clinic had concerns they would have chapped her door.

In contrast to Holland, in Finland day care is ubiquitous and of a high standard. Along with Ingrid I visited a joyous day care centre where her small son was togged up to the eyeballs while playing with other children in the snow. One morning I got up ultra-early to join in the breakfast and goldfish-feeding at a residential centre where children slept overnight, sometimes for days at a time as their parents worked night shifts or overseas. In Finland day care is taken seriously and parents have a right to 24/7 care for their pre-school children.

To explore the dark side of Finland that is connected to dysfunction and high alcohol consumption, I met Dr Jukka Makela, a psychiatrist in the National Institute for Health and Welfare. He immediately solved another mystery. Why on that January morning not far from his window in a frozen Baltic bay did men sit for hours with fishing tackle lowered through neatly cut holes? 'Ah' said Jukka, 'that is Finnish Zen.'

In Dr Jukka Makela's view there is much that is good about the Finnish health and education system and it deserves a high place on the child well-being table. But he saw two features that needed improvement. The Finns had spent decades fixating on children's technical health, but given little attention to their ability to interact. Social exclusion is a predictor of mental health problems and there are across the country 50,000 to 65,000 young people growing up excluded, unemployed and not able to take part in or contribute to society. There are also widespread concerns about the number of young children placed in care institutions and with foster families – and the quality of that care.

Even with the work of the Well Baby Clinics, there was too large a division between the work of social and health services. Autopsies in Finland of child road accident victims revealed that many had a furring of the arteries that cannot be explained by diet alone. The conclusion drawn is that these children led excessively stressful lives; they are the product of avoidant parenting. In short, the parents met the children's physical needs – but not their emotional needs.

Stress is lowest in children who are securely emotionally attached with at least one caring, competent adult: they cry out and are soothed, the parent providing the emotional scaffolding. Stress is greatest in children who appear uncontrollable and others who do not cry at all – the children of absent or distracted parents.

From 1920-40 the Well Baby Clinics taught parents not to pick children up too often when they cried, to let them cry, picking them up would only encourage them to cry even more. Being solitary and strong fitted the harsh natural conditions of Finland and its recent bleak history of civil war and fighting the Soviets.

There is a Finnish saying: 'A man will come out of even a

skinny child but not one that cries in vain'. Britain has a version of this theme: 'boys don't cry'.

Dr Makela links a stressful babyhood and childhood to subsequent excess consumption of food and alcohol. Dopamine, the organic chemical neurotransmitter in our brains, provides telling biological feedback on rewards. A rush is given by sugars and alcohol. Children who have been avoidantly parented are not at ease with themselves, other children or adults. As they get older, they self-medicate by over-eating or taking alcohol and drugs to cope with stress and anxiety. The distress they did not learn to manage in the early months and years plays out in destructive ways. In many cases, for the rest of their lives.

Alcohol and drug abuse, obesity and many heart and mental health problems are more likely to be found in avoidantly-attached children. Poor dysfunctional families are easy to spot, but for Jukka avoidant parenting was also a feature of neglectful middle-class and wealthy families who mistook material over-indulgence as an acceptable substitute for taking the time to know and soothe their children.

Avoidant parents and avoidant Scotland

A look at the child well-being table shows Finland in fourth place – thanks to high-ranking performance on material well-being, health and safety and educational performance. National and international statistics support what you see with your own eyes – there is a high standard of living and inequality is significantly lower than in Scotland. Well Baby Clinics and comprehensive day care both act in a very human way to support parents. But Finland is not perfect, it scores twelfth in the table on behaviour and risks, the type of territory that concerned Dr

Makela. His insights on children who have been avoidantly parented apply across borders.

Furred arteries, avoidant parenting and avoidant public services – Scotland and Finland certainly have a lot in common. Finland has an excuse: it used to be part of Russia and shares a border.

■

I returned to avoidant Scotland, the place where we apparently have a Soviet approach to parents and young children. Visiting Holland and Finland demonstrated that improving the life chances of children and parents is not just an individual pursuit or a futile tilt at windmills. In very practical ways intergenerational failure can be confronted, and alongside parents governments have a major role to play. Mother and Baby Well-Being Clinics, Family Centres and family nurses like Gerda help.

From achieving sanitation and clean water, an important step in public health is providing support for babies, mothers and fathers during the first 1,000 vital days. It's a step we still have to take in Scotland.

From years in senior management I know that carefully selected and applied targets and measurement can steer behaviour and organisations in the right direction. New Labour, the Conservatives and the Scottish National Party have all championed target setting and reporting on results. Adopting the UNICEF child well-being measures would help Scotland create useful targets. Working towards them would over time change personal and institutional behaviour .

CHAPTER FIVE

Before birth

The stories we tell each other about conceiving a new life probably go like this. Fall in love (or just get very drunk), move in together or get married and fall pregnant. In the womb the foetus is protected and if fate is kind a healthy baby is born and maternal and paternal instincts take over. Babies are born as blank slates with the same life chances. And any hardship can be dismissed because, as we all know, what does not kill you makes you stronger.

And what could be wrong with this straightforward picture? Quite a lot, as it happens. To understand why preconception and pregnancy are absolutely pivotal to the rest of life, it is necessary to move beyond the statistics of the last chapter that track babies into adulthood, and work with a picture of how little humans are created and develop.

At the start of this book, I advised little future humans to select their parents with the utmost care. I should now add that the best advice you can give to a woman and her partner about to conceive, is to prepare carefully for the most momentous adventure of their lives. Very roughly half of pregnancies in Scotland are unintended, unwanted or mistimed. But even with the other half, the wanted or intentional pregnancies, there is no guarantee that the parents are adequately prepared or supported.

Our common sense view assumes that newborn babies are

blank slates born 'clean' like new cars leaving the showroom. The scientific truth is that some babies have been 'clocked' in the womb. Breakthroughs in neurology and epigenetics reveal the sad truth that it is easy to inflict, however unintentionally, life-long damage on the unborn child.

Pregnancy

The time to get the foundations right around a foetus is before conception. Pregnancy is an expression of the prior life of a woman and a man. Parental code, genetic code and postal code all play their part. But first, let's revisit the story of how babies are made and grow.

Two cells, an egg-ovum and a sperm, fuse into one at conception. Our unique DNA is created and we get our genes. The fertilised egg begins to divide making many more cells that form into a round clump. Within the first four weeks – even before the mum misses her first period – outer cells in this clump have begun to form a placenta in the lining of the uterus. Inner cells, some 200 stem cells, have the capacity to form any part of the body and they multiply to form the embryo, a long tube, with the top destined to be a head and the trunk forming below. By the fifth week, the neural tube, which later develops into the brain and spinal cord, is already formed and in place.

Cells have already started to map out to form the buds of limbs, organs and muscles. With further cell multiplication and specialisation, the embryo will in a few more weeks be recognisable as a foetus.

The tiny embryo has drawn from the mum's blood stream. As it grows food, water and oxygen are delivered through the placenta. The placenta's job is also to filter out waste. But it cannot stop some waste like alcohol, tobacco, street drugs and some prescription drugs like thalidomide.

It is a myth that the womb is a completely safe haven. It isn't. When a mother smokes she lowers the amount of oxygen available to the growing baby and increases the baby's heart rate. If a woman consumes alcohol it passes from the mother's blood through the placenta to the baby. Because the growing foetus does not yet have the organs to process (metabolise) alcohol, it remains in the foetus' system much longer than in the mother's.

Weeks six to eleven are very dramatic with the foetus becoming five times bigger. It twitches. There are involuntary muscle movements and spasms. The heart throbs at 157 beats a minute. At this time the brain neither controls muscle movement nor heartbeat. Up to about week eleven the foetus gets its nourishment from the yolk until the placenta is formed.

From week 12 to week 26, tissue that will become bone is forming in what will become arms and legs and around the baby's head. The head makes up one third of the body length. Organs develop. By the end of this stage the foetus is nine inches (23cm) long. Lots of amniotic fluid is swallowed.

Around week 26 the first stimulation takes place through ears, nose and sensing and a little brain is bombarded. If the baby is to be born at that stage it could survive but with a high risk of brain damage. Over the next few weeks the brain grows rapidly and the nervous system matures. One last organ, the lung, takes shape.

In the final weeks of pregnancy the brain grows still further, the nervous system gains control over some bodily functions and the heart and blood vessels are complete. It is time to be born.

There's a good scientific argument that we really ought not to be born at this stage. Bones, a head and organs have been forming, and we have the requisite number of fingers and toes, so the basic anatomy is established. But our brains have not nearly finished taking shape, and the head needs to grow larger to accommodate this development. So nature has to send us out early otherwise we would in evolutionary and physical terms be well and truly stuck. As a result of this the human baby's period of dependence is longer than in any other species. The next step takes us into DNA, the environment and brain.

Early environment

For decades there has been a medical consensus that physical and mental health depends on an interaction between our genes and our environment. Genes 'control' the characteristics that our offspring will have. Deoxyribonucleic acid, better known as DNA, is usually located on a chromosome that controls the development of one or more traits. It is the basic unit by which genetic information is passed from parent to offspring.

Our environment in the womb comprises the oxygen and nutrition we receive, good and bad, and various stimuli based on what happens to the mother and what the mother does and does not do.

Science is moving to a new phase in understanding how genes and this environment work together. In the rapidly growing field of epigenetics, biological mechanisms are identified that switch genes on to become active and off again. In certain circumstances the environment, lived experience, has an effect on a baby's genes.

Eating, stresses and pollution and what happens round us can cause a chemical modification of our genes. It is possible for healthy genes to be switched to non-healthy genes and in turn for those genes to be passed to the next generation. Scientists have established the genetic roots for a number of diseases like Alzheimer's and cancer.

It is imperfect but perhaps helpful to think of genes and the environment (or nature and nurture) as the basic building blocks of life, like our two hands. One hand helps or complements the other while you are driving a car, opening a jar or putting on your clothes. If one hand is impaired by say a plaster cast, the outcome will be different.

This preliminary overview of genes, environment and epigenetics sets the scene for a series of critical insights on how pregnancy powerfully impacts on a baby's long-term prospects.

Programming for babies

An egg turns into an embryo, the embryo grows into a foetus and the foetus becomes a baby. Many sensitive physical, genetic changes are taking place. Can the mother get enough of the right food and water? Is she taking alcohol, street or prescription drugs or being exposed to pollution?

The risks continue as a mother's environment, and that of her foetus, is shaped by behaviours and experiences. Is the mother surrounded by good relationships, has she had good or bad life experiences, is she anxious or depressed, getting beaten up, dealing with a bereavement, facing major daily hassles like no cash – or perhaps fleeing her country? The mother's bad experiences impact on the foetus. The chemicals (stress hormones) she produces in reaction to what is happening to her reach and affect the ever-growing baby.

A good physical environment for the mother with clean water and good nutrition improve the likelihood of a good transition from egg to the formed baby. An adverse human environment, with unstable relationships, depression or violence creates deep and prolonged toxic stress. This stress is highly likely to impair the growing brain.

Starting at conception, early experiences in the womb build brain architecture in a sequential process, with simple circuits forming first as the foundation upon which more complex circuits evolve. Genes and the environment interact to shape this architecture. Genes provide the basic instructions but experiences leave a chemical 'signature' that determines whether and how the instructions are carried out. One faulty step and the risk is that the next step will not be as sound, or happen at all.

'Foetal programming' is the name given to a set of clinical observations and a theory that links the environmental conditions the mother experiences during pregnancy to health risks that the baby is more likely to face later in life. Studies have shown that a number of diseases have their origin in foetal programming including obesity, type 2 diabetes and allergies as well as behavioural conditions such as conduct disorder and attention deficit. The foetal environment is influenced by the intake of both nutrients and toxic compounds taken in by the mother. This can influence the expression of the genes and have lasting effects on the metabolic function.

Vivette Glover, Professor of Perinatal Psychobiology at Imperial College London and a prominent authority on the effects of stress in pregnancy upon foetus and child, concludes that if a mother is depressed, anxious or stressed, a child's risk of developing emotional or behavioural problems doubles from 6% to 12%.

Vivette's research on pregnant women shows that stress experienced by a mother may affect the unborn baby as early as 17 weeks after conception, and has the potential to increasingly impact the baby's subsequent development in the womb. Here's why: Cortisol, a stress hormone, passes from the mother to the foetus in the amniotic fluid through the placenta. For an adult, in the short term cortisol is good as it helps the body deal with a stressful situation. But long-term exposure to stress can cause tiredness, depression and increase the likelihood of illness.

Normally the placenta inactivates much of the cortisol passing across, thus minimising the bad effects. But prolonged exposure to cortisol may increase blood sugar levels, suppress the immune system and decrease bone formation. The function of the placenta changes with maternal anxiety through a decrease in the enzyme that breaks down cortisol. It is thought that toxic stress affects the role played by serotonin, a neurotransmitter, and that this adversely impacts on foetal development.

In a seminal report, 'From Neurons to Neighbourhoods', published in 2000, the US National Research Council and Institute of Medicine produced the results of a long interdisciplinary exercise on the malleability of the body and brain in its first moments. It subscribed to the view that genetic and environmental influences work together in a dynamic way during the unfolding passage of brain development. The diagram opposite comes from the report.

The growth in sensing (like hearing in the womb), language

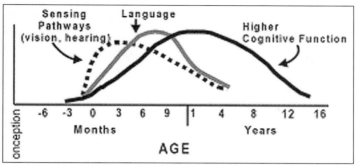

Human Brain Development – Synapse Formation
C. Nelson, in From Neurons to Neighbourhoods (2000)

and cognitive functions is weighted towards the last months in the womb and the first months of life. Note the change in the horizontal axis from months to years.

In other words the most significant time for development of the key brain functions, sensing (vision and hearing), language and higher cognitive capability (working memory, willed action and mental imagery) are in the last four months of pregnancy and up to the first and second year of life. After that growth tails off.

So neglected – so much room for improvement

There are good reasons as to why popular understanding of the pregnancy process is limited. We have no active memory of foetal life and we grow in the womb out of sight. Yet babies can remember sounds and music they first heard when they were in the womb. A three-month old baby recognises parents and regular visitors and can remember pictures and toys shown to them a few days earlier.

When you were around the age of five you could remember events before the age of three. But by the time you got a bit older those autobiographical memories slipped away. At times as adults we make the mistake of thinking that we have very early memories, when what we really have are family stories and photographs. A phenomenon known as childhood amnesia is responsible for waving good-bye to early memories.

But the fact that we cannot remember our time in the womb or the months before reaching the age of two or three does not make the first period of life vanish. Lack of conscious memory does not mean that nothing happened. On the contrary a series of life-shaping biological and neurological processes make their mark and get built into our adult bodies, brains and behaviour. What happens in the womb creates neurological and biological memory and has a fundamental impact on our lifelong well-being.

Perhaps the language and concepts wrapped around this life-giving process have become too complex. Some of the biological and medical detail might be disputed – much of this field of enquiry is in flux – and new discoveries and theories are coming to the fore. What strikes me as being clear and not in dispute is the line and logic of the story. If you do not get the first steps right, the foundations, good preparation and early stages of execution – you end up for ever picking up the pieces and trying to mend.

Farming and gardening provide a helpful metaphor. Getting seeds to germinate is tricky but the troublesome time comes next when the plants are tiny. Rain (too much or too little), temperature changes, wind, disease and a queue of slugs conspire to end or stunt plant life. In most cases once the plants have got beyond those first weeks the gardener and farmer are on a roll and vegetables and flowers follow.

If understanding about the significance of the first days is more widespread than I think it is, then as a society we are not very good at putting that knowledge into practice.

As I have already reported, each year in Scotland there are around 70,000 known conceptions and 54,000 live births. Of the 70,000 known conceptions, one in six, 11,200, (16%) ends in abortions. This is a strong sign that although the technology is available – contraception – the woman and the man are not emotionally or circumstantially ready or interested in pregnancy.

Of the 54,000 live births, 1,500 are multiple births. As we are focusing on conception, that means there are 52,500 conceptions each year resulting in one or more babies being born.

The most reliable study we have on parent's intentions around pregnancy is the Growing Up in Scotland (GUS) team's in-depth interviews with mothers who have young children. In 2013 this showed that 60% of the mothers (and partners) planned to have a child. That is the couple were conscious that pregnancy was possible and now was a good time.

A further 11,025 conceptions (16%) had not planned at all – meaning the pregnancy was an accident, the mother/father had taken a risk or contraception had failed. Whatever happened the object of the sex was not to conceive a baby.

Another 9,975 conceptions (14%) were not planned and the couple had not done anything to prevent pregnancy. The researchers were trying to capture cases where couples were not 'focused' on pregnancy but knew that pregnancy might happen because they were not using contraception.

Pulling together the 16% of women who had an abortion, with the with the 16% of women who had 'not planned at all' we find that 32% of couples, one in three, in no sense plan, never mind prepare for, pregnancy. Add the 14% who had 'not planned and had not done anything to prevent pregnancy' and 46%, close to one out of two conceptions, are unplanned.

To many women and men 'planning to have a baby' means they have stopped active contraception and are taking their chances that a pregnancy may happen. A smaller proportion of prospective parents actively take actions (starting some things and stopping others) that constitute genuine preparation. Our common language 'falling pregnant' embeds the notion that it just happens.

In the last 15 years there has been a dramatic 50% reduction in births to teenage mothers in Scotland, the number dropping from 4,700 a year to 2,300. But that still means that one in every 23 babies has a teenaged mother – a rate five times that in Holland.

Another trend named by demographers as 'differential fertility' is best illustrated by an example. Two girls Britney and Emma are born in the same year. Brittany leaves school early and has a baby at 17 years of age and another one at 19. Emma goes to university, becomes a lawyer and has her first child at 36 years of age. Britney at the age of 36 becomes a grandmother when both of her teenage girls have two babies each.

At 36 years of age Emma is 'responsible' for one child and in the same period of time, Britney is responsible for six children. One cannot conclude from this example how good a life Emma and her child will have. But an educated guess will tell you that

Britney, her girls and grand daughters will face more hardship and poverty.

The picture painted by the GUS studies is disturbing. Seven out of ten first-time mothers told GUS that they attended at least some antenatal classes and found them useful. However two out of three teenage mothers did not attend any classes, explaining that they did not like classes or groups or that they did not know where there were classes.

Across the board in Scotland one in five women smokes during pregnancy (in Lithuania and Sweden it is one in 20) and one in four drinks alcohol. Comparing the 20% highest-earning pregnant women with the 20% lowest-earners shows the spread of behaviour: 8% of the top-earning mothers smoke during pregnancy and 34% drink alcohol during pregnancy. Of the mothers in the lowest income group 49% smoke in pregnancy and only 11% drink alcohol in pregnancy. Smoking rates in pregnancy are seven times higher in Scotland's most deprived areas than in the most affluent areas. The child of a mother who smokes during pregnancy has an increased chance of infant mortality, disability, cardio and other major chronic diseases across the course of life.

Estimates of births of babies harmed by alcohol in the womb (known as Foetal Alcohol Spectrum Disorders or FASD) in Scotland vary between 1% and 3%, that is 500 to 1500 births per year. Weekend displays of binge drinking are common in city centres but the figures tell us that alcohol consumption during pregnancy is more prevalent in rural areas.

Earlier there was a statistic about higher earning women being more likely to drink during pregnancy than lower income

Scottish women. My guess is this reflects a view that 'it does not matter' or that a glass or two of wine at meals is not really 'drinking' and that the risk is only for alcoholics and binge drinkers. That's not a view supported by science.

Sir Harry Burns who was the Chief Medical Officer for Scotland put it this way: 'The truth is that alcohol exposure of any type during any trimester of pregnancy carries a real but unpredictable risk to the baby – with the eventual individual outcome neither a positive nor a negative certainty.' A senior clinician in Scotland told me of his dream of posters being displayed across Scotland of a foetus drinking vodka. Vodka was the mum's drink and through the placenta the growing foetus was plumbed into the mum's habit.

Foetal alcohol spectrum disorder (FASD) is potentially fully preventable. There is no known safe level for drinking alcohol during pregnancy. In Scotland we see the harmful effects of alcoholism passed from one generation to the next. Some of this is to do with norms and life style choices and coping with stress.

Epigenetics plays its part with genes passing on a tendency to over-consume. It is also the case that people having FASD (diagnosed or not) are less able to control their impulses, including sexual and substance misuse impulses. This contributes to our understanding of why at three years of age a group of Dunedin children lacked self-control with the prediction of a burdensome later life.

According to the 2016 Scottish health statistics 286 babies were born with a drug dependency stemming from the mother's misuse. Around 22,000 people are on methadone across

Scotland. Methadone may be better than being on heroin but that does not make it a healthy option for parenthood. Half of active street drug users are in the 16-34 year age range, the peak years for childbearing.

Research highlights an increase in domestic violence during pregnancy and following the birth of a child. It is one of the peak times for domestic violence along with separation or divorce. NHS Choices estimates that across the UK more than 30% of abuse starts in pregnancy. Official homicide figures for Scotland show that the time of greatest danger, the risk of a person being killed, is in their first twelve months of life. Expressed as the rate per million, 36 out of every million babies under one year of age were killed; the next highest group, the 31-50 year-olds, were killed at a rate of 23 per million.

Folic acid: a solution yet to be adopted
I have no grounds for being smug about pre-pregnancy preparation. I did not know then what I know now. Having got married at 40 it was seven years before we had Eva and then Thomas. This morning's cheeriness over breakfast before getting them out the door for school conceals a dark time. Before Eva we lost one baby in week 21 of pregnancy to a neural tube defect.

In the first days of pregnancy the baby's nervous system starts to develop. Folic acid (vitamin B9) from leafy greens and whole grains provides the essential nutrients for cell growth and tissue development. But it is the rarest of women who eats (or can process) enough foods having sufficient Vitamin B9 to protect her foetus from neural tube defects. Spina Bifida and other neural tube defects happen very early in pregnancy. But the risks can be reduced by 70% if women get enough folic acid in the months before pregnancy and in the first month after conception. Starting to take folic acid supplements after pregnancy is known, or at the first medical booking at weeks eight to twelve, won't cause any harm, but it will have no preventative effect either. The train has already left the station.

Our loss hurt long and it hurt hard. It took time to face the risk and uncertainty of another pregnancy but this time something was different. Way before becoming pregnant Michele supplemented her normally healthy diet with folic acid supplements. Even with five university degrees between us, our insufficient folic acid awareness caused a long dark period. In Holland messages about folic acid are printed on packets of contraceptives. If we had lived in Holland at that time or in one of more than 80 countries including the USA where folic acid fortification of food, usually flour, is mandatory, our first baby in the womb would have had a better chance of being healthy and we would have been spared the grief.

General lack of awareness, bad public policy and the fact that around half of pregnancies are unintended or mistimed make the foetus and the parents peculiarly vulnerable in Scotland. In early 2016 the Scottish Government announced its intention to add folic acid to food; yet at the time of writing (January 2018) that policy has still to be converted into practice.

Greater awareness of preparation for pregnancy is not controversial. Nor is prevention of the risk of damaged and lost babies through addition of folic acid to foodstuffs. Yet we don't do this in Scotland.

Be prepared

The language of falling in love and falling pregnant makes the passage of a new life sound like a slapstick routine. We need a new language about being ready to have a child and being prepared to have a child. It should be clear by now that the preparation has to start before and continue through pregnancy. Becoming pregnant with a smoking, alcohol or drug habit, or when suffering from depression or obesity, is a big mistake. So too is having a violent partner or not consuming enough folic acid. It is too late to fix.

Not being prepared for conception is a gamble with life. A poor hand at the start increases the odds for a poor life later. And no second hand is dealt. This is the root of so much Scottish inequality, poor health and inter-generational disadvantage. Dr Jonathan Sher, who migrated from America to Scotland years ago has been an advocate of preparation for pregnancy. He sometimes asks audiences: 'What is the difference between Las Vegas and Pregnancy? Answer: what happens in Las Vegas stays in Las Vegas; what happens in pregnancy lasts a lifetime.'

Leave ideological arguments about controlling the means of production and family values aside and think more about reproduction and preparation for life. Preparation for a new life can be an empowering decision, rather than bad luck or fate.

A worthwhile aim in Scotland is for conception to be an informed and intentional choice. The answer is to be prepared. It is too late if public services focus on the time when a woman first presents herself as being pregnant at a GP's office or a hospital midwife. But that's today's scenario in Scotland.

In the previous chapter, we saw how in Holland doctors and particularly nurses in the Mother and Baby Well-Being Clinics get to know their clients, usually women, in a very personal way and engage with their decision-making. But in Holland it is also about culture. Discussion about sex and contraception is open and upfront – surprising in a country with a Calvinist/Lutheran history. Another reason given for low teenage pregnancy is that most Dutch children can see a way forward for themselves as young adults and know that having a baby early is rarely an advantage. In short it is about what we do as a people – and what we do and do not do in our public services. Preparation must become pervasive.

Should long acting reversible contraception (LARC) be offered by the health service to women who are seriously depressed, or have an alcohol or drug problem? As a matter of routine nurses and doctors could ask women of child-bearing potential about their pregnancy intentions, such as: 'Are you likely to become pregnant in the next year?' And depending if the answer is negative, affirmative or ambivalent, prospective parents should be offered meaningful follow-up with appropriate conception counselling, care, support or provision of the LARC of each woman's choice.

For this pregnancy planning to work, as has been shown in some states in America, it helps if there is a trusted relationship between the professional asking the question and the woman giving the answer.

In our whole life course the most significant period shaping so much that follows is from being in the womb through to the first few years of life: the vital 1,000 days. Bodies and brains grow as they should. Or they don't. If the period in the womb is to be right, then the period before pregnancy needs sorting. A good pregnancy requires more than crossed fingers and a parachute jump. I put my hand up when I say that I did not appreciate this when I became a father. When I wrote '0-5 How Small Children Make a Big Difference', the significance of pre-pregnancy escaped me. I fear that the often-used term 'Early Years' is too woolly. As a group of citizens we need to do some fast learning and modify our behaviour. So do our institutions.

CHAPTER SIX
Those first two vital years of life

We sped down Glasgow's Great Western Road at 3am with Michele, in the back of the car about to give birth. Michele was in pain and panicking and I was a wreck trying to hold it together. The maternity ward when we got there was locked with no obvious way of getting through the door. A lot of loud thumping on the door, or perhaps they heard my heartbeat, and the door was opened. An hour later a little bright pink, healthy Eva was born. Within moments of being on Michele's front she propelled herself inch by inch to her breast for a feed. There was relief and joy.

Bewitched, the three of us, 16 hours later, made the journey home, put the key in the lock, pushed the door open and put the lights on. We were on our own. Eva plus car seat is put on the kitchen table. At this point Eva puckers her lips, stops breathing and changes colour. We were terrified. After a frozen eight seconds, Eva relaxed. We changed her nappy and all was well. It is the 21st of December, the winter equinox, the birth date of Eva Sinclair and Joseph Stalin. Are we up to this?

Three years later, in vigilant but more relaxed circumstances, a second healthy baby, Thomas, is born on April Fool's day. Later that afternoon we are back home.

It is an odd Scottish feature that maternity services are conducted through a rapidly-revolving medical door. One minute you are in, 16 hours later with Eva we were out and on our own. In Holland if you have your baby in a hospital you can expect to stay four or five days and once you are home the help and support of a Kraamzorg is available for eight to ten days. In Finland, with the first baby a mother will spend two to three days in the hospital and one to two days if she has given birth before. In both countries the hospital helps the mother recover and makes sure that the baby is healthy, feeding well and that the relationship is right between the mother and baby.

Attachment and scaffolding

Having children takes you to places you do not know about. I have learned that parents are caretakers who provide the structure that allows babies to grow within its protection. Eva and Thomas needed to be kept clean and fed. They both needed to be 'read' and 'interpreted': did they want some baby conversation, touch, food, sleep or perhaps just walked about in our arms at 4 o'clock in the morning until they were soothed?

We do not **own** our children, slave masters own children; parents are their caregivers or caretakers. It is our responsibility to provide the scaffolding that brings 24/7 support and guidance – and over time, if we are successful in taking the scaffolding down piece by piece, they will learn to eat with a spoon, mimic sounds, walk unaided, catch the bus, choose their school subjects, do chores about the house (with accompanying disappearing tricks and groans) and become, in their own right, independent adults and hopefully good parents themselves, with a healthy circle of friends.

Normal maternal behaviour in animals including human mothers involves two-way attachment. First is the mother to the child. This is driven by hormonal changes at the end of pregnancy and specific neural circuits in the brain. Secondly the infant to the mother, as a means to obtain nutrition, protection and comfort. Attachment by an infant can be not just to a natural mother but also to an 'allmother'.

Allmothers, a term used to describe a husband, grand-parents, siblings, nurses, nannies, baby sitters and neighbours . . . even people who set public budgets and deliver services that help support babies' scaffolding. . . was coined by Sarah Blaffer Hrdy in her book, *Natural Selection and the Female of the Species*. In the rest of this chapter and book, I will use the conventional terms 'mothers', 'fathers' and 'carers' but it would be helpful if you could keep in mind this extended notion of the mother.

Infants have a powerful desire to be close to and held by the parent or carer. A baby calls for attention by a cry. Mum picks the baby up, cuddles it, gives it a gentle shoogle accompanied by a 'goo-goo' and feeds it. The pattern gets repeated and the baby learns to make sense of the world. Life is coherent and the baby builds up trust, confidence and communication – the baby finds its way and a buffer is created against life's stresses.

In healthy families a baby forms a secure attachment with her parents as naturally as she breathes, eats, smiles and cries. This occurs easily because of her parents' attuned interactions with her. Her parents notice her physiological/affective states and they respond to her sensitively and fully. Beyond simply meeting her unique needs, however, her parents 'dance' with her. 'Hundreds of times, day after day, they dance with her,' writes Dan Hughes a therapist and academic.

There are other families where the baby neither dances nor

even hears the sound of any music. In these families she does not form such secure attachments. Rather her task – her continuous ordeal – is to learn to live with parents who are little more than strangers. Babies who live with strangers do not live well or grow well.

And what if the carer, for whatever reason, doesn't want to be closer to the child? In distracted or dysfunctional families, the cry is sometimes met with a quick cuddle or with a long nothing. Food sometimes comes and sometimes doesn't. Signals are chaotic and unpredictable. With avoidant parenting mum and dad are out, out of it or entranced by something else.

Some parents practise a way of toughening up the child by plainly turning away so that the baby does not become a softie, an attention-grabber who cries all the time and expects nothing but cuddles. Perhaps the debt collector is coming, you have had a screaming match with your partner or have a hangover: out of frustration, to prove a point, get at the partner or repeat an old stored-away impulse the baby may be hit. Or just ignored. Or hugged and loved, hit and ignored in some unfathomable pattern. The baby lives in an inconsistent and stressed world, unsure if a cry gets a sympathetic or unpleasant response, or simply nothing.

Around 300 days of the 1,000 most important days that make our world involve pre-pregnancy and pregnancy. In the next 700 days – two years – come experiences with biological, neurological, hormonal and behavioural consequences – for good or bad.

Imaging techniques such as MRI and PET scans now permit scientists and medics to carry out non-invasive examination of the brain. They are able to see the differences in the brains of young children and adults brought up with adverse social and emotional experiences, and to compare the images with those of children and adults brought up in homes where there was more consistent care and positive attention. How this comes about is that the child's brain will develop sequentially in a different way depending on its environment and experiences. A child exposed to prolonged chaotic stimulation or neglect is likely to suffer impacted neurological connectedness and, in time, less than healthy brain architecture.

Some of this is of course not new. In 1944 the British psychiatrist James Bowlby carried out a study from his case notes and published a seminal paper, 'Forty Four Juvenile Thieves, Their Character and Home Lives'. A significant minority of the children had 'affectionless character'; a phenomenon he linked through his case notes to their histories of maternal deprivation and separation.

From experience drawn from his work Bowlby went on to describe 'attachment theory'. Central to attachment is the primary carer, that person's availability and sensitive responsiveness to a young child's needs. Through knowing that the carer is reliable, the child is kept safe (whether from sabre-toothed tigers or drugged dads), forms a secure foundation and from this base explores the world.

In a secure attachment children are able to form and maintain healthy emotional bonds and relationships. Securely attached children tend to do better at school. As they mature they become more independent and empathetic, have successful social relationships and experience less depression and anxiety.

Terms like secure and insecure attachment and inconsistent and avoidant parenting might sound a bit theoretical. Instead let's talk about fear, the moment you are walking through the jungle and that sabre-tooth tiger comes round the corner. It is fair to presume that your walk would be disturbed – fear and anxiety would take over. Dr Suzanne Zeedyk, an American psychologist long based in Dundee, explains that babies have fear of impending danger, sabre-tooth tiger moments, where instinctive-evolutionary heritage kicks in and it is legitimate to feel fear.

'His fear is not imagined but is physiological and thus real for him,' Suzanne says. 'His brain knows that if he does not keep a trusted adult near him he is likely to die.'

Avoidantly-attached children (ignore them – they will toughen up) and ambivalently – or chaotically – attached children (sometimes I will feed and cuddle, other times they can just look after themselves) are more likely to be diagnosed later in life with conduct disorder, post-traumatic stress and oppositional-defiant disorder.

A two year old under the eye of a dad is busy assembling blocks on a table. On the same table is a juice that she knocks over. An emotionally healthy parent says something like, ' Oh dear, you have spilt your juice – let's clean up and get more juice' – though this time he will put it out of immediate reach. The parent stays on top of their irritation and the two year old thinks something like, dad loves me, it was an accident, he will clear up.

Replay the brick assembly and juice going flying with an angry dad. 'You are out of order. You can go thirsty and sit in your wet clothes. That will teach you a lesson.' What does the baby think this time? I am stupid and I don't deserve looking after?

Patterns like this get repeated day in day out. What a child absorbs in her brain and body about herself comes through the relationship with the parent or carer. I am loveable and competent or I am bad and disgusting. Young children reflect back on themselves the views of their parents.

Edwina Grant of Scottish Attachment in Action, a practising psychologist with distressed teenagers helped me with this example. She believes that it is through the relationship with parents that young children come to think about their feelings and learn to co-operate and share. If children have not had the benefit of a good relationship and have not learned to play, to share and cooperate at the start, their behaviour gets labelled as Attention Deficit Hyperactivity Disorder (ADHD) or Oppositional Defiant Disorder (ODD).

Christine Puckering is a child and family psychologist with over thirty years' experience working in clinical and research situations. She is the driving force behind the Mellow Ready, Mellow Bumps and Mellow Babies coaching programmes. 'Parenting does not spring from nowhere,' she told me. 'If you have never experienced good relationships, how would you form a good relationship?'

We cannot live only for ourselves. A good life involves trust and has many connections and relationships. You might remember that baby four in the maternity ward only had one visitor.

Breastfeeding

Breastfeeding has a considerable hard-wired evolutionary impact on both mother and baby. Mammalian breast milk has been engineered over millions of years to protect babies from circulating microbes. The breast and breast milk contain immune-sensor cells that tell the mum's breasts to alter the immune protective elements in the milk, often within a day or two of first baby contact with a new germ, based on the mum's large memory bank of antibodies. This next statement is probably not provable in a laboratory, but a body of thought and experience argues that the regularity, intimacy, touch, smell and internal hormonal response of the breastfeeding process help with bonding and attachment.

Worldwide medical guidelines are that all women should exclusively breastfeed till six months of age, then continue along with appropriate and complementary foods up to two years of age and beyond.

In 2005 the Organisation for Economic Cooperation and Development published results on breastfeeding at three months of age: half of all babies in Finland were breastfed, 37% in Holland and just 15% in the UK. The Infant Feeding Survey in 2010 found that 86% of UK mothers who stopped breastfeeding in the first two weeks of life would have preferred to continue, but could not obtain the support and assistance needed.

Only one in 200 women in the UK, or 0.5%, breastfeed their children until one year old, the lowest rate in the world. Only Saudi Arabia at 2% comes close compared with 27% in the US, 35% in Norway and 98% in Malawi. These figures are taken from

The Lancet medical journal that ran a series of papers on breastfeeding in 2016. One conclusion drawn by the journal was that increasing the rate of breastfeeding – greater uptake and duration – would annually worldwide prevent 800,000 child deaths and 20,000 cases of breast cancer.

Empirically demonstrated, non-controversial, protective benefits of breastfeeding for infants cover the following four acute conditions: gastrointestinal disease, respiratory disease, otitis media and necrotising enterocolitis (NEC) – a potentially lethal infection of the newborn. Other improvements regularly listed – though not always agreed in the literature – are a reduction in sudden infant death syndrome (cot death) and a reduction in childhood obesity, type 2 diabetes and, later in life, cardiovascular diseases. For mothers there is improved protection against breast cancer, ovarian cancer, diabetes, hip fracture and the alleviation of stress from having a very sick baby.

Breast is normal and it saves money. Global sales of baby milk products in 2014 were $44 billion and growing rapidly. UNICEF in a cross disciplinary report, 'Preventing Diseases and Saving Resources: the Potential Contribution of Increasing Breastfeeding in the UK' created a series of models that examined the incidence of some health conditions associated with no or low breastfeeding, along with conservative calculations of associated costs. One of their findings was that a modest increase in uptake and duration of breastfeeding would pay for itself in a year or less. And that is before going into the non-medical, human costs of sick or dead babies or the conditions that occur later in life.

NHS Scotland statistics for 2015-16 report that at weeks six to eight, in Shetland almost twice as many babies are being breastfed in comparison to Lanarkshire where 32% of babies are breastfed. Furthermore, those low rates have hardly budged in the decade and a half since standardised records were kept. Across Scotland the lowest rate of breastfeeding is among young mothers and babies living in low-income areas.

An instinct that stretches back to our mammalian past makes good economics and good medical sense today. For some women breastfeeding is physically or psychologically difficult – just not something that is done in their family or amongst their friends. As the UNICEF report shows, by a combination of training, concerted effort by midwives and health workers and peer-to-peer support that can change for the better.

What is the hard scientific evidence behind attachment?

Is this attachment stuff just conjecture and fancy words? Consider this: in July 2015 there were 11,500 children living in care in Scotland. And they had usually moved multiple times. Talk to child psychologists, social workers, police officers and primary school teachers and stories in different words of a lack of secure attachment and bonding spill out.

What counts as proof? Do we need random controlled trials where one group of say 50 babies are removed from their mothers at birth, put into a cage, fed and watered and do the follow-up to see how they get on? And compare their progress against 50 babies who have warm cuddling mothers who feed them and look after their needs?

That was precisely the experiment conducted on rhesus

macaque monkey babies during the 1950s by Professor Harry Harlow at the University of Wisconsin-Madison. Determined to test Bowlby's attachment theory, Harlow removed baby macaques (with 93% of human DNA) from their mothers. He presented the infants with the choice of surrogate mothers: one made of cloth and one of wire, in two sets of conditions. In one the wire mother had a bottle with food and the cloth mother had no food. In another the cloth mother had a bottle and the wire mother had nothing.

Baby macaques overwhelmingly opted to spend their time clinging to the cloth mother. When only the wire monkey had food, they only visited her to feed. Harlow concluded that 'contact comfort' was essential to the psychological development and health of infant monkeys and by extension to human babies.

In another experiment the baby monkeys were raised with either a wire mother or a cloth mother – both able to feed. Both sets of baby monkeys gained weight at the same rates but the wire mother's raised babies had softer stools and trouble digesting the milk, frequently suffering from diarrhoea. Harlow's explanation was that lack of contact comfort was psychologically stressful to the monkeys and the digestive problems were a physical manifestation of that stress.

Reading about these experiments creates revulsion: if you have the stomach you can find YouTube images of Harlow's baby monkeys. I have also read about but cannot bring myself to look for film on a total isolation test, involving baby monkeys who were left completely alone for various times between three and 24 months.

In the late 1980s and 1990s a real live version of this

experiment was carried out in the 700 orphanages of Romania that incarcerated 170,000 orphaned children. Professional researchers drew parallels with Harlow's experiment. True to his findings, orphaned children had more psychiatric disorders, and impaired memory, problem-solving and reasoning skills and showed indiscriminate friendliness.

Back to life as we know it
What is this mouthful I used earlier, 'oppositional-defiant disorder'? It is a condition in which a child displays continual uncooperative, defiant, hostile and annoying behaviour towards people in authority. It was precisely this condition that our front-line workers in the Wise Group were unconsciously referencing when they used the term 'starers'.

Empathy by-pass starts in pregnancy or with an abusive or neglectful carer. I once watched a man in his 20s with fine choirboy-like features being interviewed on the BBC *Panorama* programme. He had murdered a stranger in a Glasgow street. The interviewer asked if he felt regret or remorse? No, the man said, it was bad luck that the guy he stabbed happened to be walking by at that moment.

In another book in this series, *Conviction*, former police-man, John Carnochan tells the story of David the victim who becomes a perpetrator. A boy born to an alcoholic mother, shunned, shunted around, and, no doubt, punished who in time murdered a stranger in the street.

If you're struggling to accept this reality, listen to soldiers who have come back from Iraq or Afghanistan and who are suffering from trauma or post-traumatic stress. Day after day they have been out on patrol in a state of hyper-vigilance: is someone about to shoot at them, and from where? They see or take part in some terrible violence. On discharge they carry forward that vigilance, can't switch off and can't refresh themselves with a decent sleep. If soldiers get traumatised in overseas wars, is it too difficult to understand that tiny infants easily become traumatised by domestic wars or the coldness of despair?

Most mothers and fathers in Scotland do a good job of being parents. Yet at the same time they will have 'if only' moments wondering what they could have done better. This is natural. Children in care or who have come out of care frequently use the expression, 'If only my parents had been there for me'. We are all somewhere on the spectrum from being well-attached through to being avoidantly or chaotically attached.

How a mother or carer attaches with a child (and the other way about) tells us more about a child's prospects for growth and well-being than a mother's presumed maternal instinct.

Cooperative Breeders and Disposable Babies

Psychologists and neuro-biologists can tell us a lot about how children grow and the indelible markings of childhood. But they have no monopoly on wisdom.

During the second century AD the Greek physician, Soranus of Ephesus, wrote an influential text, 'Gynecology', on the care of the newborn. Among the Germans, Scythians and some civilised Greeks, new-born babies were subjected to ice-cold baths to toughen them up, and also to test them, 'in order to let die, as not worth rearing, one that cannot bear the chilling'.

For Soranus this test, but not the principle of testing, was open to question as being too stringent, as infants worth rearing could be put at risk. Yet up to early medieval times, the practice of disposing of unhealthy, illegitimate, unwanted, defective or non-viable babies was just what the Celtic, Norse, Greek and Germanic peoples did.

Testing human babies for viability drew to a close when the Christian church and the laws of the land stood against the practice. Commonplace for 10,000 years or more, infanticide became a crime in seventeenth century Britain. And so the water test of viability, the water of life, passed into baptism and the washing of the baby's head shortly after birth as the public acknowledgement of a child with a soul and a name.

David Attenborough's wildlife programmes are wonderful. But Attenborough's animals face predators, droughts and cold winters while attempting to satisfy the constant demand for enough calories to keep themselves and their offspring alive. One extra chick might be manageable, but two could endanger all their lives.

A favourite pet for children is the golden hamster. The mother cleans and protects her newborn hamster pups but she also recoups some of the investment of time and calories by gobbling up a few pups to create a litter size to meet prevailing conditions. The mother makes an assessment based on her experience. At other times animals expose themselves to mortal danger to feed or protect their young.

Mothers have, throughout time and across species, traded off between their own maternal security and the quantity and quality of offspring. Mother hunter-gatherers in particular faced daunting judgements: how can they get enough calories when they are pregnant and unable to work or collect food? Will their mate be reliable as a source of food and to protect her and the newborn against other strutting males?

Even though there have been immense changes since our ancestors were foragers, many of the basic dilemmas for mothers remain constant. A mother is at the centre weighing up a combination of concerns about what is best for her and for her child or children. Producing children is not enough, mothers have a deep desire to see their children survive and prosper but sometimes that desire is compromised.

A mother is not an island, humans are cooperative breeders and a child needs a mother or a carer. More men now embrace the role of caring. This is welcome. To borrow an old African saying – it takes a village to raise a child.

CHAPTER SEVEN
Is social class a factor?

So far we have explored the scientific evidence that many children in Scotland are damaged by adverse experiences in their first 1,000 days, and looked at international best practice in the child well-being league.

Before we can start to think about how to address such a fundamental issue in our society, it's important to understand precisely where the problem lies. I have deliberately and repeatedly used the emotive phrase 'poor parenting' to describe what I believe to be the fundamental cause of our generations of unhappy children. But what does this mean? Is it literally poverty-stricken people who are primarily responsible, generation after generation, for neglecting and abusing their kids? People who are feckless, stressed, under-educated and don't know any better?

Of course not: that would be to invite the lazy corollary, a Scottish orthodoxy, that the children from financially better-off homes will receive superior parenting and in time become successful, well-balanced, self-reliant adults. This is not true. Like woodchip paper, a good income helps to cover the cracks: it doesn't make them go away.

As I have already pointed out, the absence of a state focus on child well-being means also the absence of much useful data to tell us where we are doing badly, and where we do well. Here's the evidence that I've been able to find, first from these shores and then from further afield.

In Scotland there are two strong sources of relevant information. First, Growing Up In Scotland is a longitudinal study tracking the lives of thousands of children and their families from birth to their teenage years. Trained interviewers regularly visit the families to capture information on a range of topics. Paul Bradshaw and his team at ScotCen run the study. It is sponsored by the Scottish Government.

Secondly, is the information gleaned from the use of the Early Development Instrument. It has been adopted by East Lothian Council and the Scottish Collaboration for Public Health Research and Policy at Edinburgh University. It is widely used in Canada and Australia to provide insight at a population level to child development and also to shape interventions.

In 2012-13 Primary 1 teachers across East Lothian were given time to complete the Early Development Instrument on each newly-arrived P1 pupil. The 104-question checklist asks about the child's social competence, emotional maturity, language and cognitive ability, physical health and well-being, fine motor skills and communication skills. Each child was given a score out of ten in each category and the results compiled alongside information about each child's economic and social status.

The good news is that in East Lothian the vast majority of children – 73 out of every 100 – are, at age five, on track. But teachers have assessed that 27 out of 100 are 'vulnerable'. When a child scores in the bottom10% for the whole of East Lothian that child is judged to be vulnerable.

Is social class a factor?

Using the same assessment criteria, in Canada 28 out of 100 children are judged to be vulnerable and in Australia 24. East Lothian's performance sits between these results. Across Canada and Australia, the Early Development Indicator is used to shape state policy and service delivery to reduce vulnerability. But not here.

Looking exclusively at the group of vulnerable children, almost half came from the 40% of households with the lowest income. That means that almost half of the vulnerable children were spread through the 60% of middle and high-income earners. Breaking this down still further, the researchers found that three of these children were found in the homes of the top 20% of earners; five in the second top 20% of earners and six in the 20% of earners straddling the middle income group.

What is true for East Lothian is likely to be true for Scotland – although it has to be said that East Lothian has substantially lower rates of child poverty than many other areas of Scotland. The message is that vulnerable children are disproportionately found in the lowest income households but a significant number of vulnerable children are found across middle-to-higher income homes. By the time they reach primary school more than a quarter of Scottish children are vulnerable and risk being left behind their more settled, happier classmates.

The Growing Up in Scotland survey has found that at age five, below average vocabulary ability is found in 20% of the children from the homes that are in the top income bracket. It is worse in the homes with the bottom 20% of income where 54% of the children have below average ability with vocabulary. Problem-solving, one of the key characteristics sought by Scottish employers, is below average for 29% of the children in the top income bracket and 53% of the children at the bottom earnings scale.

In summary, childhood poverty is only modestly associated with suboptimal child development and only predicts a part of the later problems.

Adverse Childhood Experiences

In the mid 1990s Dr Felitti of Kaiser Permanente, a USA private health insurance company, gave people undergoing a comprehensive physical examination the option to provide detailed information about their childhood experiences of abuse, neglect, and family dysfunction. Felitti and his main collaborator Dr Robert Anda were trying to determine the extent to which these early influences had a connection with adults' ill health and longevity.

A total of 17,000 participants volunteered: 54% were female, 75% white, 46% were over 60 years old and 75% had at least some college education. As this was a private health insurance scheme, participants would by self-selection be higher earners.

In the study, now replicated internationally, participants were asked about ten types of childhood trauma. Five were personal: physical abuse, verbal abuse, sexual abuse, physical neglect and emotional neglect. Five were related to other family members: a parent who was an alcoholic, a mother who was a victim of domestic violence, a family member in jail, a family member diagnosed with a mental illness, and the disappearance of a parent through divorce, death or abandonment. Each type of trauma counts as one. So a person who has been physically abused, has an alcoholic father and a mother who has been beaten up has a score of three.

Around 66% reported at least one of these ten adverse experiences. Of these 87% reported at least one additional adverse experience. The most prevalent childhood adverse experiences were, in order: physical abuse; household substance abuse; parental separation or divorce; sexual abuse; household mental illness; emotional neglect; and mother treated violently.

The more adverse childhood experiences an adult reported, the higher the association with high-risk health consequences such as alcohol and drug abuse, severe obesity, promiscuity and smoking. There was also a significant correlation with depression, heart disease, cancer, chronic lung disease and shortened life span.

In comparing a person with four adverse experiences to someone with a zero score, it was observed that there was a seven-fold increase in alcoholism, a doubling of the risk of being diagnosed with cancer and a four-fold increase in emphysema. A patient with six or more adverse experiences was 30 times more likely to commit suicide.

This thorough study has become internationally established as the Adverse Childhood Experience study, or ACE. People with high ACE scores are more likely to be violent, have more broken bones, more than one marriage, more drug prescriptions, more depression, more physical malfunctions, more auto-immune diseases and are more likely to have an early death.

Public Health Wales published their own study in 2015 on ACEs based on 2,000 adults drawn from the general (not just middle class) population: one ACE was recorded by 47% of participants and four or more ACEs by 14%.

Compared to people with no ACEs, those with four or more

ACEs were four times more likely to be a high risk drinker, six times more likely to have had or caused unintended teenage pregnancy, 14 times more likely to have been the victim of violence in the past year, 16 times more likely to have used crack cocaine or heroin and 20 times more likely to have been incarcerated at some point in their life.

Dr Mark Bellis, of Public Health Wales, found that one out of three high school pupils had four or more ACEs. Having such a high number of ACEs means it is more likely that there will be a series of adult problems. But this is not fatalism – Dr Bellis also found that children with four or more ACEs are more likely to be resilient if they have a trusted adult.

Carol Craig whom I mentioned earlier has recently published *Hiding in Plain Sight: Exploring Scotland's ill health*. It is the previous book in this series and its argument and evidence are very relevant to what I'm setting out here. She grew up in a council house in Milngavie in an attractive housing estate. Real poverty was not an issue for many of the tenants yet many of her male peers have died prematurely. Carol argues that in Scotland many children's lives have been blighted by alcohol, drugs, domestic conflict, and violence. She delves into Scottish history and culture to explain why Scotland may be a high ACE country.

No full-scale research has been conducted on the prevalence of ACEs in Scotland. However, working with data drawn from Growing Up in Scotland researchers have analysed the lives of eight-year-olds and estimated their ACE scores. Two out of three children in this Scottish study have at least one ACE. These figures suggest that children in Scotland have a higher prevalence of ACEs than children in Wales. The authors looked at what the effect might be if a child was removed from a deprived area. They concluded that lifting a child from poverty would reduce the proportion of children experiencing an ACE from 65% to 51%. In short, ACEs are not just about poverty and deprivation. Children from better off homes also suffer.

At a conference in 2010 Dr Felitti, one of the originators of the ACE work, explained his method and what he found. I was stunned and after our encounter read more. Since then I have been an advocate of the revelatory and explanatory power of ACEs.The studies make clear the damage that ACEs cause and show the spread across social class. But ACEs are not like toxic stress in pregnancy or the Dunedin brain development at three years of age, a predictive tool. ACEs are retrospective, they rely on active recall. Damage to neurological and biological memory is real but not something we are aware of.

A robust picture emerges from the Early Development Indicator, Growing Up in Scotland and ACE studies. It's obvious that financial poverty imposes such severe constraints and stresses on parents that their ability to look after their children can be impaired. The children may suffer emotionally, educationally and in behaviour.

For 2015/16 after housing costs 26% of children in Scotland were living in relative poverty, (defined as a family income adjusted for family size, below 60% of the median income for all Scottish households) – a total of approximately 260,000 children. Children who live in poverty are more likely to have parents who smoke and not to have been breastfed.

Yet categorising the poor as inadequate parents does not square with the facts or the dynamics of raising children. It is economic determinism, part of a Soviet mind-set. Raising children in poverty is much harder. But framing what parents do as fundamentally a poverty issue cuts us off from a truth, that good and bad parenting runs right across different social classes. Embedded in policy and opinion is the assumption that the 'problem' rests with the poor and the feckless and a pull on the levers will do the trick. Implicit is the message: once poverty is eradicated parenting will flourish. I don't think so.

Rather than wait for the tide of income to rise, it is better to support all parents so that the children have greater lifetime opportunity and are not disadvantaged from the start.

But the more that parenting is framed as a poor person's issue, a welfare matter, the more it will be relegated to the fringe of politics, economics, health and education. Economic determinism (little money = a squalid life, lots of money = a good life) does not reflect what we see happening around us every day.

Let's be frank. There is a large-scale denial about the struggle of middle-class and wealthier parents to raise children in today's Scotland. It's easy to say that the problem is 'over the wall' with the poor and feckless. In the time that it took me to write this chapter, I had the following encounters with middle class parents and children.

- An Edinburgh business colleague talked openly over a long walk about the depression, anxiety and self-harm that took hold of his daughter in her late teenage years. His wife took cold comfort from the fact that so many girls self-harmed in the secondary school where she taught.

- A friend in his forties talked about his brain fog and

stress and that of his sisters, stemming from an accountant father who was alcoholic and violent. To illustrate he told me a story of his dad stopping the car, pulling his mum out and giving her a beating.

■   My sister told of a friend who had just discovered that her respectable, religious husband had for years been sexually abusing the daughter – he fled and the daughter was in a mental health ward under 24 hour observation.

It is men who sexually abuse children, not men above or below a certain pay grade. Child neglect and outsourcing of children to nurseries can be two beans in the same pod. Spoiling children and pampering them to within an inch of their lives is an easy route when you have a busy schedule and a buoyant bank balance. According to the Growing Up in Scotland study, 34% of the highest-earning mothers drink alcohol during pregnancy, more than any lower income group.

The tales nurseries reveal
I have visited a lot of day nurseries: favourable impressions are mixed with unease. One nursery worker expressed a sentiment echoed by peers, 'I often come out of the baby room and wonder, just what are we doing?'

And then there is parent behaviour. 'I have no issue with the wee mums,' a nursery worker said. 'They come to talk about their children and what the children have been doing that day. They listen to what we have to say. It is the big mums that are the problem, they don't want to hear or are too busy.' A nursery worker tells the story of explaining to a mother, who is a GP, that her child had a speech delay. Back came the reply, 'Is that not what YOU are supposed to get right?'

Inez Murray is the former owner and manager of the excellent Four Seasons nursery in Glasgow. She cared about the nursery and her staff and cared about each child and what was good for them. At £12,000 a year per full-time child it is more of a financial commitment than most middle class parents can afford.

'Children show us what is happening at home,' said Inez. Many of the parents are so highly driven that she wonders why they had children in the first place. Her husband who helped out at the nursery conjectures that if they were open on Christmas day, there would be a small queue of parents at the door. For some parents children seem part of the 'veneer' of life, an extension to the 'perfect' house.

Inez had a series of brave conversations with parents about setting boundaries, redirecting attention or investing time in their children rather than spending guilt money. On my last visit Inez was about to have a conversation with a pushy parent about over-expectations.

In a trend that may be bad for business but good for the children, 90% of the Four Seasons' preschool children now come part-time. Ten years ago it was the other way round.

Not on the 'to do' list: orphans with parents
Working women with children are consummate jugglers. Paid work needs to be done to afford the next supermarket shop or the next house. There is commuting, an overbearing boss at work, food to be bought and cooked, some sort of domestic cleanliness to be maintained, elderly parents or in-laws to be cared for, older children to be picked up and dropped off at netball and football, tantrums managed (or ignored if it is the

partner) and the children's bed-time routine completed. All this before checking emails and falling into bed wondering if there are enough ironed clothes for the morning. For some women it is needs must. For other women it is about doing justice to their education and fulfilling their potential.

High-flying husbands catch the occasional domestic juggling ball but leave the house early, return late or are away days in London or further afield. Men and women who excel at work have busy schedules, get promoted, do more work, travel further and have business dinners. It's compulsive and addictive.

People tend to marry their own type and two high-achieving parents can easily get into this harum-scarum pattern. In the Growing up in Scotland study 38% of the top quintile of educated parents (that is the 20% of parents with the highest education) report parental stress. The only group of parents to report higher stress at 46% are the bottom quintile of the least educated parents. In between these two groups, parents report stress averaging 29 – 36%.

Most frequently it is men who get into job overdrive and the mother becomes in effect a single parent. And what if the child is a bit difficult or different? Does pride and busyness allow you to recognise or tune in and give that extra support or does denial set in? Dads when they come back are too tired, drunk, have too many other things to worry about, are on the internet planning the next ski-trip and need to get up early in the morning.

'Sodding-off' by mums, dads or both can be a feature of affluence. 'I needed my mum and dad to be there for me' is a repeated refrain from children who have experienced a blighted childhood, 'and they were not there'. Children know when they are not on the 'To Do' list. A smart address, leather booties, designer baby clothing or later electronic gizmos and a fee-paying education may assuage parental guilt, but 'stuff' does not substitute for consistent loving and sensitive care. Parking children out of sight does not fit with the practice of attachment.

A good friend brought up in one of the most expensive parts of London told me about her many advantages but how she grew up not feeling loved. 'In some families' she told me 'you can do anything. In my family it was the opposite, I was stupid and it was assumed that whatever I tried would not work.'

In some families the performance measures are set: exam passes, sporting achievement and musical ability. And that is it.

Edwina Grant of Scottish Attachment in Action, whom we met in the previous chapter, puts it this way: 'Building the bonds of secure attachment between parents and children is vital for every aspect of healthy child development; it's an investment and major protective factor for the teenage years.'

Close to the top of America's wealth tree and one of the top five schools for Science, Technology, Engineering and Maths scores is the Henry M Gunn High School in Palo Alto in Silicon Valley. Parents sacrifice to get into the catchment area for the school. A place with the coolest gadgets, brightest minds and optimism, the pinnacle of a meritocratic elite excelling in studies, music and sport.

Except for one thing. In the last ten years this high-flying school has had a suicide rate four or five times above the national average. It is true that suicides come in clusters and are complex. 'The amount of stress at our school is ridiculous,' said pupil

Martha Cabot on YouTube after one of the suicides. 'Students feel the constant need at our school of having to keep up with all the achievements. We love our moms and dads – but calm down.'

An American clinical psychologist, Madeline Levine, practises in Marin County, one of the most affluent areas in America, just across the Golden Gate Bridge from San Francisco. She was propelled to write a book, *The Price of Privilege*, after a bright, personable, 15 year-old girl with affluent, adoring and pre-occupied parents, left her office. The girl had rolled up her sleeve to show how she used a razor to incise the word EMPTY on her left forearm. This was a girl with seemingly everything. Looking through her appointment book, Madeline saw more children whose life fitted the same pattern: affluence and material advantage, great pressure to succeed and little connection with or empathy from the mother or father. These were unhappy and disconnected teenagers, empty on the inside and full of wealth on the outside.

David Cameron at seven and Boris Johnson a little later were sent to preparatory boarding school before boarding at Eton. However good your early attachment might be abandon-ment and the swapping of a family relationship for exposure to institutional neglect and abuse cannot be a good idea. My sorrow extends both to them, the 'privileged' looked-after children and the rest of us, who suffer from their damaged emotional makeup.

At Arizona State University Professor Suniya Luthar has been researching economic and social class stratification and child pathologies. Her conclusion is that at each extreme, the poor and rich children show unusually high rates of dysfunction.

In particular the children of rich parents (earning over $200,000 a year) had a higher rate of alcohol and drug abuse than poor children and much higher than the national norm. Clinically significant depression, anxiety or delinquent behaviour was two to three times higher than the national average. There seems to be a U-shaped curve in pathologies amongst children that is shaped by socio-economic status. She has identified two causes of distress amongst the children of rich parents: pressure to excel academically and in extra-curricular pursuits, and a feeling of isolation from their parents.

Communication about staying out late, alcohol, what friends are doing, drugs and sex is hardly likely to start in the teenage years if the trust has not been established much earlier.

Before you come after me and ask, what type of parent are you? I raise my palms and acknowledge that I can on occasions be an ignoramus and a bad-tempered grump (a reference is available). Parenting is not about perfection – perfection is a fantasy land on the road to sadness. Parenting in real life means having a messy house and messy emotions with bucketloads of time devoted to the everyday and out of which joy emerges.

CHAPTER EIGHT

Crisis is the time to change direction

As I hope I have demonstrated so far, the hard-pressed public sector in both Scotland and the UK spends a huge amount of our national income on coping with the entirely predictable consequences of poor parenting. The government does what governments (at least in this country) usually do – tackle the consequences of a national crisis rather than its causes.

This cannot go on. It is morally wrong not to deploy the proven solutions and processes that other nations have successfully used, to turn around our parenting performance. And it fails the common sense test in view of our dire need for the skills required to improve our sagging productivity and economic growth. The Scottish economy needs more employable, competent, stable people if it is to achieve reliable growth in the decades to come, particularly in view of the likely damage to our skills base if Brexit happens and the flow of EU migrants upon whom we depend is slowed. Look at the Scottish budget figures and you can see that there are more commitments on the table than there are available funds. Schools today cannot afford books for their classes: senior civil servants and local government officials are focused on cutting costs further.

The screw turns further
Scottish society and its labour market are changing in a slow yet profound way. More people are living into very old age. Already the NHS gasps and splutters as it attempts to live within

its budget. Health is the single largest area of devolved expenditure in Scotland. We are facing a rapid increase in funds required to treat more elderly people with multiple medical and care needs. By 2031 Scotland's population of 65 years plus will rise by 62%, and the 85+ group by 144%. By 2040, if current conditions prevail, there will be a six-fold increase in the number of people living beyond 85 years compared with 1990. This massive additional demand on a struggling healthcare system is exacerbated by the fact that around 80% of lifetime health expenditure currently comes in the last two years of life.

Over the same period the size of the Scottish workforce is due to shrink. Currently three people in work support through taxation and possibly their income, one older person. In twenty years this ratio will become 2:1. With fiscal devolution meaning that 50% of government revenues are directly raised in Scotland, this picture of costs relentlessly rising while our capacity to earn goes down is not a happy one.

An emerging human and financial crisis creates the conditions for a sober rethink and a shift of priorities. In my working life I have found that a crisis focuses minds and harnesses effort. Crisis is the time to park tinkering and shift direction. We can't do the same as we always have and expect different results.

To address such a fundamental national challenge means resetting our priorities, as citizens, parents and government. It's all too easy to blame government for our state of affairs, but that's both unrealistic and unfair. In a democratic society, governments tend to reflect the values and philosophies of the electorate – and I believe that's the case in modern Scotland.

What government, parents and citizens do, what the mood music is and what our expectations are, all need fundamental realignment with the reality that our poor parenting skills comprise both a national crisis and a huge opportunity to rebalance our public sector cost base with substantial potential savings. This is a long-term endeavour to create a society with greater well-being and a more robust economy.

Making the best use of public expenditure
Improving the relationship between parents and children has short-term cost implications. But in the grand scheme of things, not too much money needs to be involved. As we invest so little now, a small increase in investment will go a long way. Today's babies if properly looked after are tomorrow's carers, workers and taxpayers. If we don't change today's neglected and trauma-tised babies will tomorrow need caring for, be unemployable and a liability on the national exchequer. And these costs can be enormous as we saw in those dramatic statistics about Scotland's looked-after children.

What it is tempting to define as Scotland's Parenting Crisis turns out to be a huge and complex issue about economic efficiency, productivity, equality of opportunity, social cohesion and the quality of life.

To understand this better it helps to dig into investment, rates of return and well-being. Let's start by revisiting the work of Professor James Heckman, director of the Centre for the Economics of Human Development at the University of Chicago. As mentioned in Chapters Two and Three, Prof Heckman is a Nobel Prize-winning economist who discovered that the best rate of return that a society could make was from early investment in parents and children. Conversely the lowest rate

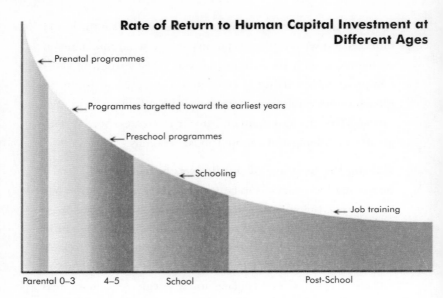

Rate of Return to Human Capital Investment at Different Ages

← Prenatal programmes

← Programmes targetted toward the earliest years

← Preschool programmes

← Schooling

← Job training

Parental 0–3   4–5   School   Post-School

of return came from investing in later life. The big gains in human capital formation and development came way before primary school.

Through investing in parents and early years an annual rate of return of between 7% and 13% per year is achieved and continues to be achieved through life. The returns flow through the lives of happier, better-adjusted, more employable young people who demonstrate improved school attainment, reduction in crime, reduced alcohol and drugs abuse, better physical and mental health and taxes paid from jobs. Young children who receive this investment are more likely as adults to get a job and not end up on welfare. If government wants to decrease inequality and increase productivity, the direction is clear.

Heckman summarised the findings in the diagram above.

Table 2:
Public Spend on Education for year 2014/15

Average University place in Scotland	£9/10,000
Average Secondary place	£6,790
Average Primary place	£4,810
Average day care place for 3 & 4 year olds	£1,700

(Source: Angela Constance MSP Parliamentary Answer 16 March 2016 on the average cost of primary and secondary place – Audit of Higher Education in Scottish Universities, July 2016)

Institute of Fiscal Studies, Long Run Comparison of Spending per Pupil Across Different Stages of Education, February 2017, Chris Belfield and Luke Sibieta)

Along the bottom line is age from before 0 years to 21 years of age. On the vertical axis is the rate of return from investment. The biggest rates of return come, in order, from pre-birth actions, then 0-3 years of age and the smallest rate of return is at 21 years of age.

The rate of return per pound of investment made while a person is young is higher than the rate of return for the same pound made at a later age. This applies across the economic spectrum. Successful remedial work for young people coming out of a dysfunctional environment becomes progressively more costly the later it is attempted. The earlier the intervention the less costly and the more effective it is for our society.

Heckman's findings fly in the face of how tax money is spent in the UK and Scotland. As shown in Table 2, most money per head goes to university education, then secondary school, followed by primary and last of all pre-school. In health spend it is the same – with little being spent on the first 1,000 days and most being spent on the last days of life.

Currently we spend our hard-earned public money on health and education in entirely opposite ways to where the greatest rates of return are found. We invest more by age and body weight than by rate of return.

'A major determinant of successful schools is successful families,' Heckman told his audience in Edinburgh. 'Schools work with what parents bring them. . . Scottish skill formation policy should be based on this basic principle.' It costs schools more to fix or try to fix problems created earlier and the outcomes are not as good. Earlier is better.

Skill formation is dynamic; skill begets skill, motivation begets motivation. Success breeds success and failure begets failure. Digging behind the long-term data sets of early intervention programmes, Heckman found no evidence of sustained improvement in participant IQ. What had improved were 'character' skills: self-control, openness, and ability to get on with people, determination, sticking to task and empathy. These behavioural and life skills – along with intelligence – determine economic and social success. They are the very soft skills or attributes that were found most lacking among the Wise Group trainees and which employers told Future Skills Scotland they most needed. Too much education and skills policy focuses on academic skills partly because these can be measured and that is what we have done before.

Participating in work
Over the last few decades between 12 and 16% of young people aged 18 to 24 were not in work, training or education. In policy

circles this is known as the NEET group (Not in Education Employment or Training). The sad fact is that if you can't find a way ahead in those few years after leaving school your prospects for the coming years are bleak.

This is not a happy prospect for the young people trapped in jobless-land and is an added cost to the people who work. To get this in proportion, yet again we find that the highest public sector spend is on older people (pensions, health and care costs). But the NEETs are a group of people with unfulfilled lives, a cost to other people. If we had our priorities right in Scotland, these people would be working and contributing their talents and tax.

In eighteen years with the Wise Group, I watched different governments' stick and carrot approach change. Invariably, the stick got bigger and the carrot smaller. When I started the offer was to provide a minimum wage for training and work experience for up to one year. By the time I left the basic offer was for a maximum of six months and, instead of a wage, you were on benefits plus £10 a week – with a matching reduction in how much we could spend per person on training. Our average age of recruit was 21 years old. When I moved on, what should have been an incentive was being used as a stick – if you did not join the scheme your benefits would be docked.

At 21 years, the average age of a Wise Group long-term unemployed person, I was still at university, where I spent four years with fees and a grant being paid. I found this hard to square – why were the most able receiving the biggest subsidy, while those who struggled the most on short rations were pursued as malingerers, workshy and scroungers? The support on offer to young and long-term unemployed people was, and is, too little too late. Around every two or three years programmes are changed in name and design to help conceal previous failure. Without really trying I have just jotted down ten programmes started and disbanded in the last thirty years: Employment Training, Youth Training Scheme, Community Programme, Youth Opportunities Programme, New Deal, Flexible New Deal, Futures Jobs Fund, Work Programme, Enterprise Allowance and Employment Zones.

Yes, some people do play the system – but so do some middle class people and corporations. Threatening to take away every person's welfare benefit is a strange way of stopping a few dodgers. The argument is that an economic incentive (pull and push) is what is needed to mobilise the long-term unemployed. An economic incentive might work for me or for you but if you are in the slough of despair, it is as much help as installing loud speakers in areas of high unemployment and blasting out on the hour, 'Pull your socks up'. It is not going to help the neglected or abused and people with mental health and addiction problems. If the assumption of rational economic man is to work, your life has first to hang together.

What is needed is engagement, listening to and building up trust and confidence. The long-term unemployed 21 year-old did not become cut-off at 21. Unemployment is not spread like rain equally across the population; it is significantly more concentrated in some households. As trade or shipyard jobs were once passed down the line from father to son, so is unemployment now passed down from mothers and fathers to sons and daughters.

The Wise Group starers cannot be good carers. In today's tough workplace many, but not all, are essentially unemployable.

Post-school programmes are inadequate and come too late.

It is not just common sense but a researched conclusion that public spending triggered by remedial action is always more expensive and less effective than getting it right first time. Enhanced parenting is more effective than supporting damaged children in later years.

'Early investment in the lives of disadvantaged children,' Prof Heckman argues, 'will help reduce inequality, in both the short and the long run.'

It's not difficult to see why investing in early years is right or why it is a good in itself. And economically in terms of rate of return, productivity and participation in the labour market, it is the best course of action.

Political commitment and Implementation Deficit Syndrome

Investing in the first 1,000 days might be the right thing to do – but why do that when there are roads to be built, old people to be looked after and police to be deployed?

'When it comes to opportunity, we won't entrench the advantages of the fortunate few,' said Theresa May on entering No 10. 'We will do everything to help anybody, whatever your background, to go as far as your talents will take you.'

Gordon Brown told us, 'The great and unacceptable concentration of poverty amongst households with young children is the greatest indictment of our country in this generation and the greatest challenge of all.'

'Tackling poverty and inequality – and improving opportunity for all – will be my personal mission as your First Minister,' said Nicola Sturgeon in 2014 at the SNP national conference where she took over as leader and First Minister.

Resist being cynical about leaders such as May, Brown or Sturgeon: they mean what they say. Their job is to set direction, make big decisions, hold their tribe or party together and win elections. It is too easy to blame politicians; it is too easy just to go round looking to blame someone.

Blair and Brown introduced Sure Start community-based day care for young children, and working families tax credits that largely helped people in work with young children. Nicola Sturgeon rescued the health visitor service when she was in charge of health and more recently has ramped up day care. However Sure Start has all but disappeared under David Cameron and Theresa May and the health visitor service is in a tailspin in England. In Scotland the Early Years Collaborative and the National Parenting Strategy have all but disappeared into the long grass.

In the absence of a consistent and nationwide focus on the first 1,000 days, I suggest we are looking at a failure of our system of civil society. Why is it so hard for government to recognise the inescapable truth behind so many reports, studies and data that warn we are proceeding implacably down the wrong road when it comes to child well-being?

Just as we have come to see that more and more children are presenting at school or their GPs with attention or hyperactivity disorders, so I conclude that there is in Britain and Scotland a matching adult disorder which I label the Implementation Deficit Syndrome (IDS).

IDS afflicts citizens, officials and politicians alike. It

comprises two familiar symptoms:

- Being locked into doing what we have done before, even when we know it does not work

- A lack of will, skills and dedication to follow through a new initiative or strategy.

I first became aware of the existence of IDS when I worked on employment at Scottish Enterprise. I then saw the condition reappearing when investigating what happened to the seminal 2011 report by the Christie Commission on 'The Future Delivery of Public Services'. It made the case for early intervention and preventative public spend and it recommended empowering individuals and communities by involving them in designing and delivering better services. Government departments were charged to review their work through this lens and the Finance and other Holyrood Committees set to work. It was then the 'in' fashion but sadly proved to be short-lived in implementation and impact.

I asked James Mitchell, the Professor of Public Policy at Edinburgh University and a member of the Commission, why so little progress had been made in delivering on its recommendations despite the Scottish Government having accepted their priorities? 'People want to do the right thing,' he told me, 'but there are two problems: vested interest and targets.'

Take the education system. Universities and schools look after their institutional self-interest and that extends through their boards, management and the trade unions that represent their staff. Professor Mitchell has observed universities manoeuvering for an increasingly unjustifiable slice of Scottish educational spend.

For example when I had a senior position in Scottish Enterprise I found that with respect to education and training, robust elbows and a blind eye were more effective than evidence. I made a presentation to the Scottish Enterprise board about the link between soft skills and early years. One of the board members, then Chief Executive of the Scottish Funding Council for universities and colleges, was notably silent. Weeks later walking to the station with him, he opened up and confirmed that the big gains in education were in the earliest months and years. He was knowledgeable, gave me helpful references to follow up and added, 'Of course you are right but I can't be seen to say that.'

In education, health or local authorities, once funds have been allocated, a gravitational pull is created that then exerts pressure to spend that cash and get more.

'Real' men (and women), the ones at the top, are there to manage their resources, meet their targets and protect their patch. It's called 'producer capture' when the interests of the senior management in an organisation reflect their own particular interest rather than those they are supposed to serve. Producer interests then take over and they are not aligned with the best interests of the consumer or citizen. This mixture of vested interest and producer capture is the scenario we face in our public bodies – and it's why long overdue change is not happening.

'There is nothing more difficult and dangerous, or more doubtful of success, than an attempt to introduce a new order of things in any state,' wrote Niccolo Machiavelli, the Secretary to the Chancery of the Florentine Republic in 1500. 'For the innovator has for enemies all those who derived advantages from the old order of things, whilst those who expect to be benefited by the new institutions will be but lukewarm defenders.' James Mitchell tells us that the modern (Scottish) interpretation is that targets lock organisations and people into what they are already doing. 'There are not enough rewards or incentives to encourage prevention and early intervention,' he observes.

His point is that if, for example, more staff and therefore expenditure were directed by the NHS to support the first 1,000 days, the benefits would be reaped elsewhere – improved school performance, a reduction in crime and a reduction in human suffering. The early investor, in this case the NHS, would gain no direct reward. Its management would be unable to claim targets achieved or budgets saved, with the likely personal benefit that would then accrue. Additional pressure against change comes from within the NHS where each interest group or Royal College defends its patch, and each community defends its hospitals from closure.

Gus O'Donnell, the former head of the UK civil service, has argued that we should measure the well-being of children with the same rigour that we assess academic achievement. 'Starting young, if we measured the well-being and resilience of our children at schools,' O'Donnell has written, 'our chances of having less remedial work to do with them in later life – through the courts, mental hospitals and social services – would be greatly enhanced.'

I would argue that we should start earlier than schools, but you get his drift. You also wonder why, as the head of the civil service, he was not able to unlock this particularly important door?

Add the intoxicating effects of the short-term vested interests and the wrong targets, and we see in front of us the array of obstacles to reform. Here's a story of basic human psychology at work.

Marshmallows and delayed gratification

At Stanford University in the early 1960s an experiment was carried out that has since been successfully repeated on many occasions. Pre-school children between the ages of three and six were offered a choice, a deal. The children were told they could take one marshmallow now, or if they waited, they could have two marshmallows. A researcher left the room and observed from outside before returning 15 minutes later. YouTube film showed the contortions of the children as they resisted or caved in.

Around one third of the children managed to delay gratification. Following them into adolescence and early adulthood showed that the children who delayed gratification were more capable and socially skilled. Statistics testify they had higher test scores and lower substance abuse and obesity than the children who lacked self-control: echoes of the Dunedin exercise mentioned earlier in Chapter Three.

At the Wise Group we could not explain why Friday absenteeism was shooting up. We floundered and then discovered that while our bank had instructions to pay wages on Fridays, in practice the cash hit accounts about 9pm each Thursday night. A lot of our people got hammered, had their one marshmallow and could not come to work the next day. We sorted timing with the bank but could not do much about delayed gratification – or lack of self-control.

The public point the finger at the City for the short-term recklessness that got us into financial meltdown in 2007-8. In the UK and Scottish political election cycles, rolling news and party positioning steers politicians and public sector managers to favour the immediate, the urgent over the important. Political decision makers want to see results (marshmallows) now, living as they do with the fear that they will be humiliated by the tabloids and judged to be asleep on the job if there are no short-term results. It is hard to resist this pressure, even if it means only one marshmallow. Sugar rush rules.

It's also a factor that Ministers are not omnipotent: they have to work with the crooked timber of the government machine – their own colleagues with their own agendas, civil servants, health boards, and local government. I experienced this at first-hand when I worked with Labour Ministers on the New Deal and employment issues between 1998 and 2004.

It was the same from 2009 to 2012 when I was the unpaid advisor to Noel Dolan, principal advisor to Nicola Sturgeon, then the Health Minister, and I was trying to get the issues raised in this book acted on. While events like the financial crash and its knock-on effects rumbled on in the background, I was aware of how the short-term kept barging in: the urgent over the important. At one critical time all attention was on the Asian flu scare.

And as we worked through tangible initiatives such as Health Visitor Numbers, Family Nurse Partnership and Baby Boxes, I felt a tension between what could be directly delivered and had voter appeal and the longer term, more systemic initiatives to fund mother and baby well-being clinics – the clinics that the

Dutch have in every neighbourhood that is only a pram push away and where you know the professionals and they know you. Even as the Health Minister you are constrained by budgets and what the government machine can deliver.

'In choosing our investments we should follow the evidence about what works and then stick to our course for the long-term. When investing in people, by far the highest rate of return comes from investing in our very youngest,' wrote Stephen Boyle in a newspaper article. Stephen was the Head of Future Skills Scotland and is now Chief Economist of the Bank of Scotland. 'Passing the marshmallow test (is) all the more important for Scotland. We are already a rich and successful nation, close to the top of any global league table. Yet income per person here lags 30% behind the best performers. We could be £10,000 per person per year better off if we were more productive. As well as more money in people's pockets that would mean the opportunity for more generously funded public services.'

Framing what needs doing

How an issue is framed significantly affects what follows. The same actions by a baby could be framed as either: this baby is just being bad, wants too much attention and is testing its luck; or the baby is screaming because he is fully awake and wants some food and loving care. How baby behaviour is framed, or perceived by a carer, has significant consequences for how the carer responds.

Framing is equally important in public policy. Donating organs save lives – countries where most lives are saved presume that on death an organ can be transplanted. If you do not want to donate your organs you have to explicitly opt out. Countries where organ donation is at its lowest, like the UK, require an opt-in. Lives are lost and saved through subtle issues like framing.

In Scotland and the rest of the UK, the critical issue for babies and parents has been framed as day care. 'We already deliver 16 hours a week of free childcare for all three and four years olds as well,' Nicola Sturgeon said in the same conference speech quoted earlier. 'From August next year, that entitlement will extend to 27% of two year-olds as well. That is more hours of childcare than in any other part of the UK and we should be proud of that.'

Now, this was a big political commitment and it's one that is being delivered – though how it is going to be paid for is still being fought over. Holyrood (and Westminster) equate early years and parenting with good quality day care. Both governments advance four sound reasons to support quality (and quality really does matter) childcare:

- The most deprived and at risk children who go to nursery benefit the most from the security and stimulation of day care.

- The best way of lifting low-income households out of poverty is by making it easier for one or both parents to go out to work without having their gains in pay taken away by childcare costs.

- Across the board it helps parents to cope and the children to become socialised.

- Women in our culture take on most of the responsibility for childcare and day care plays its part in allowing them to fulfil themselves.

Day care is the answer to the question: how do we help parents with young children get to work and make sure a job is worth the trouble? But we need to ask ourselves whether this framing represents the right question. Surely the more important framing is: how can we best help all parents during those critical 1,000 days from conception to two years, to become better at the most demanding role they will ever face. . . and the one with the longest-lasting national consequences.

In Holland, at the top of the child well-being table, very little state investment goes into day care. The investment is in Mother and Baby Well-being Clinics and Family Centres, under-pinned by a strong culture that includes part-time work and a supportive lifestyle. In Finland where 24/7 day care is available, parents are given the choice between sending their children to day care or getting a state subsidy to look after their own children at home.

We need to ask ourselves the simple question: why should the state subsidise parents if they put their children in institutional day care – but not support the same parents if they look after their own young children at home?

Day care is too late if a child has already been damaged in the womb and in the first 24 pre-nursery months of life. And even if a toddler joins a nursery, the nursery provision is for 16 hours a week. So what conditions and behaviours face the child for the other 152 hours of the week? Nurseries could be empowered to do more to help parents to cope and to develop a healthier approach to parenting. Multiple studies have shown that the most effective early interventions (like Perry Preschool) have three legs: working with the child, working with the parent and working with the parent and child together. It is stretching it to think that regular day care in Scotland embraces this approach.

Scottish children who regularly 'dog' school come from traumatised, chaotic and vulnerable parents. Children of nursery age with the most toxic stress or baggage are the ones least likely to turn up – and if they enrol are most likely to drop out. Nursery school dropouts are already disruptive, have poor language and cognitive development. Some will go to bed hungry.

A side-story illustrates this point. Kate Reid retired some years ago as Director of Education in Lothian Regional Council. In the mid 1980s Kate moved back to Scotland and, as her own children were maturing, she moved back into work heading up a youth initiative in Lothian's education department that wanted to transform the prospects of children destined for the NEET group.

Instead of designing some grand-sounding top-end strategy, she went local and dedicated all her attention to one rough-and-tumble school in Armadale, working with 32 pupils who caused teachers to pull out their own hair. She worked intensively with each child. Got under their skin and took the trouble to visit their parents at home. 'They were neglectful parents,' Kate explains. 'But they were very proud of their children.' In time some of the parents responded to Kate's concern and became more involved in their children's progress, although others stuck with their despair.

What puzzled Kate was why these children were only now, towards the end of their secondary schooling, being identified as needing special help. Why had this not been picked up before?

So off she went into tracking back through primary school records and, where they existed, at nursery school.

Her troubled youngsters of today were described in nursery reports as 'Young for his age.' By P1, 'He can't sit still and was immature.' The degree of culpability increased so that by P3, 'He refuses to do what he is told. He is a disobedient boy.' And by the end of primary school war has broken out: 'This boy is out of order. He is aggressive and nonconforming.'

Kate Reid discovered a mass of assessments, all properly written down and filed away but with no recommendations as to what should happen next. It was like discovering a mass of doctors' diagnoses and a professional disconnect when it came to the follow-through remedial steps. Emotionally the children were crippled, being battered or ignored at home and castigated and shunned at school. She coined the term, 'the Fat File Syndrome' to explain this phenomenon – a close relation of Implementation Deficit Syndrome.

Kate Reid's story provides an example of the need to engage and stand by parents right at the start. The need for professional therapeutic support can be identified at two and three years of age. It makes no sense to wait until the child becomes an adolescent and has more severe attainment, mental health and behavioural needs. Keeping a score and sending young people to the Children's Panel is not the answer.

To be blunt: if we want more people to work, improve productivity and have greater equality of opportunity in Scotland, more parents need to do a better job. More needs to be done to help parents do a better job. This is a legitimate role for public policy and public investment.

Blaming parents does not help them or their babies. Most pregnant mothers and mothers with babies are hungry for help. Holland and the other countries at the head of the table are not communist or fascist states trampling over the rights and choices of parents. Nor are they waiting for society to be more equal and then all will be well and parents will automatically be better. Parents are ultimately responsible for their own children. The role of the state is to prepare and support mothers and fathers to stand on their own feet and manage to be good parents – it is no more complicated than that.

However the Scottish conundrum will turn into a full-blown crisis if we think that increased day care and a seven-minute GP appointment are the answer to today's embedded parenting challenges.

Governments can clearly help with parenting and early years, but which way round does it work? Do governments lead or follow public opinion? Government will not support parents and early years investment unless the people want it. Do you remember offices and pubs being filled with cigarette smoke? After smoking in public places had been trialled in Ireland, the Scottish Government tested public opinion and found that by a large majority the public endorsed the idea of a ban. So within a short period what once seemed impossible became inevitable.

Keep to task in reform of public services: predict, prevent, intervene early and help people to help themselves

What we have considered as intractable social and health problems are realistically over time manageable and open to improvement. It is not about pulling the levers of power and sending a vast train-set of services whirring in another direction, in the process taking over what parents do. It is about helping parents to help themselves.

In Chapter Two I told the story of my Wise Group days and the approach we adopted of putting the responsibility on the long-term unemployed to find their next job. A government auditor subsequently chastised us – the leavers told the auditors that they had got the jobs through their own efforts. There is a queer difference between empowering a person, helping them to stand on their own feet and the too common model of consumers of public services being passive recipients.

Cultural change is needed. Many different cultures make up Scotland: children in care, teenage mothers, young long term unemployed, graduates making their way in the job market, parents who drink too much alcohol, well-off parents too busy to notice what is happening to their children and more. Different cultures need different types of help – the mix of what they can do for themselves and what the state can do varies. One size fits all when it comes to buying an umbrella but not when it comes to turning round parenting culture.

Ultimately it is about what parents know and do particularly before and during pregnancy and the first period of life. Before the Scottish state becomes more supportive I believe it will need to find a bigger community of interest to give government a push and to keep it on track.

Scotland has a long way to go, to move from tolerating to loving children. Enlightened parenting practices are the norm in most neighbouring countries. Twelve out of the thirteen countries that score highest in child well-being are nearest to us including Holland, Norway, Iceland, Finland, Germany and

France. These are easy places to visit and, as I found, their child well-being specialists are happy to share their knowledge and experiences to folk with a hunger to change things for the better.

CHAPTER NINE

Optimism

As I hope I have made clear, there are many good things going on within Scotland. Real people are dealing with real problems and creating real opportunities for their children, often against the huge odds that life has dealt them. Public institutions have shifted up a notch. Voluntary bodies and charities have developed valuable support services for parents and their babies that often draw parallels with good practice in the countries at the top of that UNICEF league.

What follows are some non-religious parables. We have much to build on.

Patricia and John

Owen and Gerry's story starts before their current parents Patricia and John came into their lives. It was Glasgow New Year and time for a raucous night. Owen was ten weeks old and Gerry was three years old when their parents threw the party.

Their older half brother and sister slipped out of the house, wandered along to the local police station and asked for help. This was more than a night that got out of hand. The house was chaotic and dangerous and the police and social work took the two older children into care and left the two young ones with their mum and dad. A pity for Owen and Gerry, as it was the older children who looked out for them.

Four months later and Owen and Gerry were taken into

emergency care, released back to their parents and then taken into care again. By the time Owen was ten months old he had been uprooted five times before being put in a foster home with Gerry for the next two years.

What about Owen's birth mum? Why could she not hear and respond to her own children's cries? What burden did she have from her own past, tucked away and unresolved? She had a dim memory of being an infant, a ghost from a past that told her she was left for hours alone at home. Her stepfather had a cruel explosive temper, thrashings followed and his friends came into her bed when she was twelve. Owen's mother was burdened, reaching adulthood with deep unhealed wounds. She found it hard to care for herself and her new partner was an echo of the past. How was she to care for her children? These were children destined to live Horrible Histories.

This thumbnail portrait of Owen's birth mother is a decent guess. All of us are caught up in our own pasts. Inheritance is more about what our parents do to us as children and what we in turn do to our own children, than a few family photographs and an old sideboard. It is common when raising children to feel and hear our own parents' 'voice', a voice and a way of doing things that come from a long way back.

Just before Owen turned three Patricia and John took the brothers into their home as foster parents, with a view to adoption. 'Adopting is for life,' Patricia tells me. 'Making a relationship is a life-long commitment. The majority of adopters go to the end of the earth for their children.' They have gone further than Arctic explorers.

Two years after taking the boys into foster care Patricia and

John opted to adopt. The birth parents contested the adoption and it took three years of stress, uncertainty, courts and social work reports before Patricia and John became the permanent, legal parents.

Patricia and John knew that all was not well with Owen and Gerry. One would think that the law and public services would be rallying to their aid. It took eight years of being on the case to get a diagnosis and support for Owen. He has a learning difficulty, is dyslexic, hyper-vigilant and impulsive.

Owen has trouble going to bed and staying in bed. Instead of his bedroom being a soft spot, it caused anxiety and fear. Patricia and John wondered if Owen was attention-seeking and trying to exert control over them. Later in therapy Owen unearthed an early memory of repeatedly going to bed and being hungry. Installing a stocked mini-fridge in his bedroom has helped ease the strain, provided comfort – just in case.

Patricia and John love Owen's humour and growing ability to socialise. At times he has been moving along and doing well. Currently when they come home from work they find Owen perched anxiously on the windowsill waiting. His mum and dad are finding it difficult to support him – he sees himself as being worthless, is withdrawn, finds it hard to get up and even the simplest of tasks is too much. There is so little semblance of order in his bedroom that he now answers to 'Captain Chaos'. At the moment he is not bouncing back.

Gerry has learning difficulties but managed to hold down a job for the past three years. A year ago there was tension over his girlfriend, Gerry walked out of the house and stayed away – but he is now back.

As a family they have grown up together, eaten round a table, laughed and joked, had holidays and gone through the school years. They are together for one another, tensions and all. This is a good news story. People like Patricia and John get no recognition, no building is named after them and when you walk by them in the street you would not know that they had been to places where famous explorers don't go.

What happened to the older half-brother and half-sister, taken into institutional care? Owen and Gerry have contact with their half-sister, but they now keep the link from a sense of duty. Their sister has considerable issues of her own. After spending many years in prison for a very serious crime their half-brother was released but is now back in prison.

We owe huge respect to Patricia and John (not to overlook Owen and Gerry) and other foster and adoptive parents in Scotland today for possessing superhuman powers of love, patience and dedication to the children that they bring into their lives. Repeatedly, they pick themselves up and bash into an unsympathetic system of rights, law and procedures that does not give due regard to attachment. Owen moved to five different carers in his first ten months of life.

Isabel Nelson and the vital years before school
In 1973 Isabel, her husband and four young children moved from an awful privately rented tenement into the Hutcheson E block in the Gorbals. She felt set up for life in her new spacious award-winning flat a short walk from Glasgow city centre.

Within five weeks mildew appeared on the walls and spread. A partial electrical heating system could not heat up concrete wall panels. Isabel pitched herself into what became an anti-dampness campaign to take on Glasgow City Council. Over time all of the thousand plus tenants were re-housed and the blocks demolished.

Fifteen years on, having done her first O-Grade in 1975 and gained a lot of savvy from the campaign, Isabel enrolled as a mature student, got a degree from Glasgow University, worked as a researcher for an architectural professor on dampness and insulation and joined me in Heatwise Glasgow. We worked closely together for twelve years. Isabel has through the years been a Liberal activist and stood for parliament. 'My campaign experience turned me to politics,' she explains, 'because I had witnessed how a group of individuals could change things.'

With Isabel being long retired we met at the funeral of an ex-colleague who died in his 50s (a lot of our people died young). Isabel in a very motherly fashion set about dusting me down, cleaning white marks off the arm of my black coat.

Having not seen one another for 15 years we caught up over lunch. I mentioned my growing interest in the first period of life. 'Early years is easy, Alan,' Isabel told me, 'I played with them on the floor, drew pictures, read stories, sang and took them to the library.' This task was not made any the easier by her husband being an alcoholic.

All four of her children did well at school and now have good jobs and families of their own. Her reward is seeing them and being woven into their lives and those of her grandchildren. Three of the families live ten minutes from her house and, until recently, Isabel joined them in the caravan holidays in the south of France. The fourth member of the family lives in England, has a small business, comes up regularly and Isabel helps him with book-keeping and VAT returns.

While the children were very young Isabel was there for her family. With four small children and no one in work, hers would have been one of the financially poorest houses in Scotland. Though more money would have helped, Isabel was able to give her children what they needed most.

Effective Pre and Primary School Evaluation (EPPE) selected at age three 3,000 children from across all sectors of society to provide long-term information on their development. First the researchers interviewed parents and carers, found out about parental income and education, collected data on birth weight and participation in play groups and childcare centres. Judgements were made about the quality of the childcare the children received and later about the quality of the teachers at primary school. At ages five and eleven the researchers tested the attainment of each child on literacy and numeracy.

These are major predictors of attainment later in life. At age five the most significant influences on literacy were, moving from smallest to largest effect: gender – girls better than boys; birth weight; social and economic class, mother's education and, most significant of all, 'Home Learning Environment'.

So what is this Home Learning Environment? It is about what happens in the house before school age: reading, teaching songs and nursery rhymes, painting and drawing, playing with numbers and letters and going to the library.

'It is easy Alan,' recalls Isobel. She knew what to do and was able to do it. It is interesting that she was unwittingly echoing the conclusions of a large carefully constructed study of children – it is what parents do in those vital early years that matters. And that should not be confused with the size of the bank balance.

143

Neil Williams and the fight for his son

Many years ago an old coal-miner pointed to a field and told me of the antics of pit ponies brought up the shaft to daylight and grass after months of confinement in the foul air and pitch darkness of the coal tunnels. The ponies staggered, ran, kicked, rolled and threw themselves about like dervishes.

Neil Williams' son Josh was taken into care at 18 months. It was judged that neither parent could properly look after him. For the next six years, in between children's panel meetings and foster care arrangements, Neil met Josh for one hour twice a week in an office with two social workers observing.

A safeguarder was appointed to determine what was in Josh's best interests and held two outdoor sessions with Neil and Josh. 'It was a different story being outside,' Neil said. 'We cuddled, gave each other high-fives and played football.' It was Neil and Josh's pit pony moment and it set Josh on the way to having a chance.

Neil is in his mid-forties and is in his own words, 'a big lump of a guy, happy-go-lucky and no oil painting'. He grew up in one of Glasgow's big council housing estates with a caring mum and two brothers; his own dad was not around. On leaving school he was a trainee sewing-machinist and for the past ten years has held a job in distribution. He was just off a shift, still wearing his overalls when we first met.

Through work Neil met Anne and after six months being together she became pregnant with Josh. 'She was never a mummy person,' Neil explains. The house was 'like a toilet'. At the time Neil thought she was lazy, but now he has come to realise that Anne had mental health problems, most likely postnatal depression. Strains grew – Anne would go out leaving baby Josh alone in the house or with a 14 year-old girl in the street. By the time Josh was four years old, Anne was bringing men back to the house.

Neil alerted the social work department and confronted Anne. Anne accused Neil of assault. He was arrested and banned from the house and the street. Social workers removed Josh from the house and he spent his Primary 1 year staying with foster parents. Neil now had a new identity as an unfit father, a wife-beater and a drug abuser. Tests showed this last charge not to be true; the other charges were harder to shift.

For Neil the stress was horrific. He could not walk away from Josh and he now knows that he could have done things differently, but he was at a loss. For Josh now aged six, three foster homes followed over the next 18 months. At the first home Neil managed to telephone Josh on Christmas da. But that was it, access was restricted. In foster home number two all seemed good on the surface but in a house with other children Josh was bottom of the pecking order and it did not feel right.

During this second foster home period, Neil got access to Josh – with an observer in attendance. Josh kicked out saying he wanted to be with his dad and was very clingy. Josh also came to meetings badly bruised and with a black eye. The explanation from the foster parents was that he had fallen over while walking and eating an Empire biscuit. Neil had many sessions with social workers and the Children's Panel. He complained, made his case and knows that he sometimes lost his cool.

Foster home number two gave notice that they were terminating Josh's stay. Josh moved to foster home number three, 'a god-send', where they really looked after and cared about the now seven year-old.

Weighing up all the evidence the Children's Panel was inclined towards Josh being put up for adoption. The safeguarder mentioned earlier was appointed and came down on the side that Neil should be given a chance if he could prove that he was now a fit father.

Neil had clashed with the social workers, knew he was not a perfect dad, was in a total muddle and desperate to be with Josh. As Neil flapped about, one of his brothers was very supportive but more was needed. Then a stroke of luck: he met Lorna from Parent Network Scotland. Neil is sure that, 'Lorna did not think I was for real'. Face to face for an hour each week for three months she helped him to understand his own behaviour and what it took to be a good father. In the contact hours with Josh he tried to put into practice what he learned. It helped. A book Lorna gave him at the time, *Bringing up Happy Children*, still sits next to Neil's bed.

Anne became more stable and did not contest Neil's move to have sole custody of Josh. Over a two-month period, through a combination of observation of Neil and Josh together, written work and interviews, social workers put Neil through a parenting capacity test. What will you do with Josh when you are at work? If Josh throws a tantrum in a shop what will you do? If Josh does not do his homework – what will you do about it? Neil passed – and father and son were back together.

Neil's employer agreed to change his shift pattern so that

he could walk Josh to school in the morning. They have a laugh on the way. For Neil, it is one of the highlights of his day. His work-mates have given Neil a pat on the back for what he is doing. Josh is now nine and has loads of friends at a school where he is thriving. Recently Josh had a meltdown at school but the school understands and Neil feels that they are on his side and that of Josh. Life is all go for Neil, it's very demanding but he loves it. Financially it is hard.

More has come out from Josh about the abuse he received in the second foster home. Of course Josh should never, in Neil's eyes, have had to deal with the stresses that he has confronted in his young life. But that is where they are. Neil can deal with it. 'I owe them so much. Without the support of Lorna and Parent Network Scotland, I really don't know what would have happened – I dread to think.'

Parenting Network Scotland is a very small charity that runs 'Parenting Matters' small group courses and peer to peer activities and supports people like Neil. I was so struck by what they do and their potential that I recently joined their Board of Directors.

Ann Hume and the olive branch

It was late in a November afternoon and Ann Hume, who leads the Olivebank nursery in Musselburgh, calls in a friendly voice to a dad leaving with his little daughter Olivia; 'Frank, what are you cooking for your tea tonight?'

'I am doing bolognaise,' comes back the reply and they are on their way.

Just the normal exchange you would expect, until you find out that the staff at Olivebank had been really worried by Olivia's slow weight gain. Through home visits they got to know the family and realised that Olivia's, and for that matter her parents' diet consisted of potato and then more potatoes. A helping hand was given in going to the shops and taking the parents through the preparation of macaroni cheese, soup and the afore-mentioned bolognaise. Olivia's mum has a learning difficulty and the dad has his own issues and a basic job.

Earlier I played with a two year-old girl who was busy organising shapes on a little desk and chattering away. She seemed, apart from eyes that were not quite right, normal to me. It turned out that her mother was a heroin addict and, as heroin passes directly from the mother into her baby's blood stream, her first days of life were taken up with cold-turkey detoxification.

Inside the nursery there is a calm atmosphere and outside, on this bright winter afternoon, half of the children are playing on the grass or scooting about in trucks and tricycles. The play area is alive with fast-moving children and staff keep an attentive eye.

Back inside a little girl is in construction mode but it does not go according to plan and her frustration breaks out. Within seconds she is off the deep-end shouting, launching the shapes across the room and sweeping everything off the surface of the desk. With impressive patience and calm, as though someone has said pass the salt, the unflustered nursery worker soothes and chats and over the next six or seven minutes the toddler returns to earth and resumes playing.

East Lothian Council set up and financed the Olivebank Child and Family Centre. Its aim is to help 50 vulnerable children and their parents and carers through day care, support, home visits and parent groups. It also means getting involved in helping families with the rest of their lives – from social workers, to the court system, Children's Panels, debts or the craft of shopping and looking after the house.

Ann Hume and her dedicated group of young and not so young women are making a difference in the wilderness of family life commonly thought to be beyond reach. After two years of support a mother can clearly be seen getting on the floor to play with her child. TVs are turned off at home. There is engagement with a three year-old expelled from a 'normal' nursery. A relationship is established with a mum who has fallen out with a string of nurseries. There are light bulb moments with a child: he is not trying to manipulate you, what is happening is normal – he likes you and wants your attention.

And all the time funding comes and goes. A day group, a toddler group and a dad's group were set up with the charity Children 1st and its alcohol and drugs initiative. The funding ended and Ann's team is determined to try and keep the group's work going. Ann and her team are not alone. There is a small scattering of family centres across Scotland that engage parents at the deep end bringing some peace to life and preventing an escalation of troubles. They perform an immensely valuable service that could be expanded where they work and across the country.

Jack and Isla: supporting young mothers

I found myself in a block of flats in Dundee, sitting on the floor. Crawling over to meet me was nine-month old Jack. He let me know that I had to hold out fingers which he grabbed with his whole hand, pulled himself up and made wobbly-legged steps round me with the greatest big grin on his face. Twenty minutes later he was in his room and fast asleep – the flat was calm and it became easier to talk to Isla his mum. Not that talking to Isla was difficult: she is a very warm young woman of 20 with a no-nonsense way.

Susan, a health visitor who now worked in the Family Nurse Partnership programme, was also in the house. Through a text message Susan had made contact with Isla when Isla was 14 weeks pregnant and still living in her mother and father's house. Her brother no longer lived there. He had been in jail for a long number of years.

When I sat on Isla's living room floor she told me she had known Susan for about 15 months. They had a strong relationship but not one easy to categorise. Susan is not a substitute mother – Isla has a mum. Nor is it that of a nurse confined to dealing with the nuts and bolts of maternal and child health. It is a respectful, intimate relationship. Later in the afternoon when Isla mentioned something she wanted to do, 'We will talk about that,' said Susan, 'later'. They nodded at each other and would return to the topic without me being there. Isla has worked since leaving school, and wants to get a job again even though she can't imagine leaving Jack,

It was the relationship that got me, more than the catalogue of stuff they had worked through: debts and budgeting, boyfriends – past and prospective – social services, food and Isla's over-weight state, Jack's feeding, sleep and constipation. Susan was one of Isla's first visitors when she gave birth in the Special Baby Care Unit.

'I have friends – but I do not trust them in the way that I

trust Susan,' Isla told me. 'I can talk to her about anything. I understand what she says.' At the crux of Isla's life is her relationship to her own parents. They live nearby and are a source of both support and tension – a normal scenario for a 20 year old but heightened because of Isla's child and the parents still seeing her as their little girl. In their view she can't manage on her own, they want control and have demonstrably strong views on how she should look after Jack. Their strong opinion is that Isla should have stayed at home.

Isla wants her independence and to raise Jack in her own way. What Susan saw was, 'a capable young woman who had outgrown her parents.' Now Isla waits until Susan visits and would talk over what her parents told her to do.

Susan feels that when Jack goes to school he will be one of the 'together' kids, ready to get on having side-stepped many of the hurdles Isla was working her way through. 'Jack has changed my life for the better,' Isla tells me. 'I love spending time with Susan and learning about what is best for him.' It works for the mother and it works for the child.

Turning back intergenerational turmoil by this method costs £3,000 a year per mother and the intervention is timed to run for 30 months – six months of pregnancy and the first two years of the baby's life. Could the programme be better targeted? Will the evaluation commissioned by the Scottish Government show that over a lifetime the Family Nurse Partnership provides value for money? Or that the existing health visitor system if boosted could provide the continuous and respectful relationship that turns a struggling life around? I do not know but I can tell you that it costs costs £33,000 a year to keep Isla's brother in jail.

Matt Forde and his many children

Matt Forde is at 59 a slightly less hairy and slimmed down version of Santa Claus (I know him well enough to make bad jokes). For 25 years he worked in residential care and youth justice. In time he became a senior social work manager before heading up the National Society for the Prevention of Cruelty to Children (NSPCC) in Scotland, a job he has done for the last seven years. He exudes a quiet dedication; his sense of optimism is alive.

He argues that relationships are what matters in early childhood. Yet, there are practically no services around the country that have professionals with the skills and knowledge to nurture and promote healthy attachments. 'First and foremost,' he tells me,' there is nothing inevitable about child maltreatment, it can be prevented.'

'We are working in Scotland to flesh out how we can meet the aspiration to improve children's well-being. There are many people and organisations striving to make a difference, but it's not easy to see what will deliver the change,' Matt says. 'We decided to develop services that harnessed the most important evidence coming from a burgeoning body of scientific research on children's development. That evidence has been translated into effective services, tools, interventions and campaigns that make a difference at the level of a child and family.'

For example since 2011 Matt has been running a trial of the New Orleans Model for maltreated infants in foster care between the ages of zero and five in cooperation with Glasgow City Council and NHS Greater Glasgow and Clyde. It is the largest infant mental health initiative of its kind in the UK. First developed in the USA, it helps social workers and children's hearings decide whether a child should return to their birth family or be permanently cared for by an adoptive family. NSPCC workers assess the relationship and attachment of a child with both the foster carer and the birth family. They then formulate a treatment plan for the parents, and most often a support plan for the foster carers too.

The birth parents learn to care for their children, those that they get back or others they may have in the future. The norm is that once they have had a child removed birth parents are left with their problems, while the foster or adoptive parents have to push for support. But under this trial, after intensive treatment and support for the birth family that may last for up to nine months, a recommendation is made to the children's panel on the child's future home, be it with the adoptive or birth family.

NSPCC combine three methods to help birth and foster parents. First, a 'Circle of Security' that uses attachment theory to create better parent-child relationships and build a more secure base from which the child can explore. Second, 'Parent-Infant Psychotherapy' to improve the ability of parents to reflect on their child's needs and provide a more secure relationship. Third, Video-Interaction Guidance; parents are filmed doing what they normally do with their child. Feedback is given that builds on what the parents do well, helping them to see how they can improve communication and relationship with their child.

A randomised controlled trial of some services run by Glasgow City was started in 2011. Definitive findings will in time emerge; research ethics and good practice prohibit speculation on the outcomes. In New Orleans where the original work took place there was a large reduction in repeat maltreatment. A seven-year follow-up study showed that children who went through the programme, whether they went to the birth home or to adoption, had the same mental health and well-being outcomes as their classmates. That's a remarkable outcome when you consider the normally poor outcomes of looked-after children. The birth parents themselves also show evidence of fundamental change, whether they get their child home or not, because very often the relationship they develop with the staff in the infant and family team is the first nurturing relationship they have ever experienced.

Our looked-after children system in its design is blind to the crucial importance of attachment. The Scottish Children's Reporter's Administration research into permanency planning for children removed from their birth parents found that, for the majority, it took more than two years from a child's first involvement with social services to achieve a permanent home with carers or foster parents. No fewer than 13% of children experienced four or five placements. In 2015 across Scotland there were 15,400 children in care. Children in care compared to their peers are six times more likely to have a conduct disorder and four times more likely to have mental health difficulties. Some children in care do go on to have good lives as adults. But a massively disproportionate number become teenage mothers, the homeless people you see on the street or do not see because they are in jail. Our system looks like a modern form of slavery.

Matt and his colleagues run two other programmes on infant mental health in the community and both have accompanying random controlled trials. Minding the Baby, developed in Yale, works with vulnerable young first-time mums from six months on in pregnancy to the child's second birthday. A social worker and health visitor work together to support the young family, helping with practical aspects of childrearing and using the tools described earlier to improve nurture and encourage reflective parenting.

One of the nurses at the NSPCC Govan centre told me about supporting a young woman with a messed-up family background. She got to know the young woman during the pregnancy and met the father. He was not reliable. After the birth it was the nurse who visited and supported the woman and not the dad. He promised to reduce his use of drugs – it did not happen. His unpredictability continued: once when the mother left the baby alone with him she returned to find a very distressed baby. Was it harm? Was it neglect? Did the baby fall? That incident was a tipping point for the mum. She made the decision that she would be better off without the father.

Parents under Pressure is an intervention offered to families with substance problems where there is evidence that treatment has led to some stability. It works in a time-limited way, relying heavily on video-interactive guidance alongside practical help with managing money and life skills. Matt and his colleagues have been struck by how often 'light bulb' moments have occurred that help parents keep a sense of calm, be more sensitive and caring.

All three of these interventions work at the tough end where parenting is truly under stress. Once the Scottish Government is persuaded to direct resources to preventing life problems rather than chase 'emergency spend', it will have some solid ground to walk on thanks to Matt and the NSPCC.

About a year ago I was catching up with Matt. With his face glowing he told me that he and his wife had just adopted a very new baby. His older boys are growing up and his wife was young enough to meet the adoption rules. I congratulated him and told him of my admiration – we joked about decking the house out with baby gear and the years of plastic that follow and sleepless nights. 'It is OK,' he told me. 'So many friends of my age seem to need to fill up their time by flying on budget airlines to Berlin. I don't like flying.'

What did I learn?

The alchemy, the magic within the everyday business of bringing up and nurturing children is the responsibility of parents and families. Many Patricias and Johns, Neils and Isabels are hidden away. We should be careful to recognise the brilliant work that is going on around Scotland to help mothers and fathers improve their parenting skills, and prevent another generation of babies from growing up damaged and stunted.

CHAPTER TEN
A road map to better child well-being

It helps to begin with the end in mind. That must be to build a country where each and every child has a real chance of a decent life. 'Scotland should be the best country to bring up children in the world.' How can this aspiration be converted from, at best, a politician's simplistic wish to a practical measure of our performance in the international child well-being stakes? Before embarking on a journey it helps to know where you are now. Are we getting better compared to our peers, flat-lining or getting worse?

Put simply, our new national priority must be to ensure that Scotland moves up that telling UNICEF league table to attain a top ten place, alongside the likes of Ireland, Denmark, Belgium and Switzerland. There is no point in setting our collective sights any lower: other countries have shown the way. We can build on the good work going on now and be inspired by what we see elsewhere in Europe.

A big reduction in the personal misery of children and parents alike, and in the process a reduction in intergenerational pain, would be the primary benefits. Happier children and parents, creating a less stressed and more cohesive society, will be the big win and we must not lose sight of that overarching human objective.

Better preparation and better parenting will bring substantial benefits to our society and economy. Children will be ready for school, classroom chaos will go down and attainment go up, violence will reduce, mental and physical health will improve and productivity increase. We will have a more cohesive society. Public expenditure will be better balanced with more spent on the important and less on the urgent.

If there is a better route to greater well-being, to a happier, more productive Scotland, I have not stumbled across it. To achieve this we need to be able to better prepare people who are likely to become parents, and then support them better through those first vital 1,000 days from conception to two years old. It sounds simple, it makes common sense – but how on earth can we achieve such a daunting objective in today's complex, interlinked society where culture, what people do, is embedded across peer-groups and when government is increasingly cash-strapped?

Let's dream a little. Let's set down some thoughts on what a road map to better parenting for Scotland could look like, for starters, for discussion and serious consideration. Our parenting predicament deserves nothing less.

The first challenging step on to this road map is for Scotland to accept that it has a national parenting crisis that urgently needs tackled. I don't underestimate the difficulties that recognising this unfortunate reality will cause a variety of people, from politicians to civil servants, from health service leaders to local authority councillors, academics to trade unions, commentators to parents both actual and prospective, and religious institutions to voluntary bodies. But I do hope this book provides a helpful start for all of these vested interests by presenting this case in as factual and unemotional a manner as I can.

The second, equally challenging, step is to develop a long-term map and to follow that map to move Scotland up the UNICEF table. By 'long-term' I mean a timescale that spans parliamentary cycles, decades and generations. This is obviously not a quick fix issue. Look at the countries at the top of the child well-being league and you will appreciate the huge effort that was required over many decades – and the efforts they are making today to be even better.

The third challenge is to know where we are and how we are doing. UNICEF's index of child well-being offers a ready-made benchmark. To refresh your memory, the index described in Chapter Four comprises 26 indicators taken from five categories that make up well-being: material wealth to deprivation, health, education, behavioural risks (fertility, alcohol and cannabis use), housing and environment. It's therefore a priority to create the datasets and measurements that would give us much-needed clarity on where Scotland truly sits in the international league of child well-being. At present all we know is that the UK is in 16th place, in the bottom half of the table, and we have assumed that this is a reasonable proxy for Scotland.

But that may not be true: indeed one gains a sense that while we may be doing better in some areas, there are surely others where we lie at the bottom of the UK heap.

I tried in my research for this book, working with good friends in the economics and statistics world, to construct a ranking for Scotland using the UNICEF criteria, which would show where we stood separate from the whole of the UK. The work that needed to be done was beyond our limited resources, for not only would we need to have a handle on the appropriate and up-to-date Scottish measurements but we would need to know the self-same data for the rest of the UK and all the other countries in the table. Had I kept at this task, I would not have finished this book.

The UNICEF child well-being table gives us a snapshot of one period of time – childhood. We know from research quoted in this book that toxic stress and adversity in pregnancy and early life is a strong predictor of poor adult physical and mental health. Scotland's adult health record is dismal.

We have some measurements which are not in the UNICEF table but which act as indictators of future life prospects and they deserve greater attention. These include rates of teenage pregnancy and uptake and duration of breastfeeding.

There are some new figures that need to be collected clinically or compiled through reliable surveys and acted upon (no more fat files please). These include:

■ How many people prepare well for pregnancy?

■ Toxicology screening results (for alcohol and drug dependence) in obstetrics and for the newborn.

■ How many children in the 18-36 months age bracket have poor brain health?

■ How many children's non-attendance or 'drop out' rates at nursery flag a concern?

Formidable, surely but impossible. . . ?

Where to start?

In the short term some parents-to-be and mothers and fathers of young children (and the allmothers) can engage with what we now know about the significance of the first 1,000 days and reflect on what it means for them.

Decision-makers and managers in the public sector might be surprised at the current patchy but encouraging number of initiatives and projects working on relationships and preparation for parenthood and alcohol and drug programmes. As I outlined in previous chapters the good news includes health visitors and a range of enterprising voluntary organisations from the large national bodies like Barnardo's, the National Society for the Prevention of Cruelty to Children (NSPCC) and the much smaller organisations such as Mellow Parenting, Parent Network Scotland, and With Kids. These all work to prepare and support struggling parents. This enthusiasm and expertise can be built upon. I apologise to the public and voluntary organisations I have not mentioned; I do not want this chapter to read like an address list.

If we could achieve short-term wins in the form of measurable improvements and changes in direction that would be encouraging as well as helping to guide the next stages.

The foundations of a long-term programme

But let's look more widely about what should be done, and is within the competence of the Scottish government to deliver – a child well-being programme.

■ **Take preconception seriously**

Help children in primary school understand what sexual abuse is, what behaviour is acceptable and what is not. Where necessary make it easy for children to talk and get support. If I had not merged into the background and watched NSPCC facilitators run a session in a primary school to help children gain the words and knowledge to protect themselves and where to turn for help if needed I would not have appreciated the strength of this exercise.

Barnardo's have been running PATHS in 13 schools across Scotland. This programme improves school children's social and emotional learning skills. Mellow Parenting has run "Mellow Ready' with young people and in women's prisons. I am not trying to be exhaustive here. I only want to demonstrate that it is possible to act.

The government could also ensure that health workers routinely ask men and women of childbearing years about their pregnancy intentions, such as, 'Are you likely to become pregnant in the next year?' They could examine ways of offering support in developing individual Reproductive Life Plans for 16 to 30 year-olds (the average age for a first time mother in Scotland is 28).

In March 2016 the Scottish Public Health Minister announced her intention for Scotland to proceed with mandatory fortification of flour with folic acid (Vitamin B9) to prevent miscarriages, stillbirths and other consequences of neural tube defects (such as Spina Bifida). Neural tubes are the part of every foetus that should develop into the brain and spinal cord. Specifically, the Minister requested that Food Standards Scotland investigate the benefits, potential risks and any other obstacles to Scotland adding Vitamin B9 to the flour supply.

In August 2017 (no hurry here then) Food Standards Scotland responded to the Minister in two seemingly contradictory ways. On the one hand, Food Standards confirmed that its Scientific Advisory Committee on Nutrition had reviewed the latest international research and once again unequivocally recommended folic acid fortification, as already happens in nearly 80 countries around the world. For many years, the UK has required the addition of thiamine, calcium carbonate, iron and nicotinic acid to flour – but not folic acid. On the other hand, the agency argued that introducing foliates should not be done in Scotland alone as it was too costly to act before the rest of the UK. If this were an exam paper, in red ink, I would write, 'Could do better'.

The government should also ensure easy, speedy access to counselling for men and women who abuse alcohol, drugs, are violent or have mental health problems. This would enable them to make more use of the Long Acting Reversible Contraception (LARC) of their choice while they are attempting and being assisted to resolve their immediate and underlying problems.

■ Support mothers and fathers with a new baby
In Holland the introduction of a Kraamzorg mother's help at birth costs £875 for five days at five hours a day (this is a 2013 figure but it won't be far out from today's cost). If that support were extended at that cost across all the 54,000 births a year in Scotland it would cost £47 million a year. If made available only to the one in four at-risk families it would cost £12 million a year.

Save the Children in their report 'Breast Feeding: Policy Matters' compared five developed countries and their breast-feeding policy and practice. In 2010 the UK had the highest rate of 'early initiation of breast feeding' (70%) and the lowest rate of 'exclusive breast feeding rates under six months' (5%).

Breastfeeding has been framed in Scotland as a life-style choice and formula feeding has become normalised. There is a clear divide with mothers on low or fixed incomes using formula milk and financially better-off mothers breastfeeding. Within minutes and days of birth health inequalities become embedded.

Corporations can be berated for promotion and advertising of baby formula products. It is a big worldwide market. In the same Save the Children Report the charity points out that in 2006-2007 the milk formula marketing budget was ten times that of the UK Government's spend on promoting breast feeding. Save the Children and others believe that in hospitals the baby milk industry comes close to breaking the rules and codes of conduct. Scotland can guard against this and provide timely help for mothers to assist with breastfeeding and put resource into building peer-to-peer networks.

All parents and children will benefit from investment in the infrastructure of support to meet the scale and complexity of parents' needs. A basic network already exists of midwives, Family Nurse Partnership workers and health visitors. There is one Family Nurse Partnership Nurse to every 25 young mothers, which is a demanding but a do-able workload. But for a conventional health visitor the ratio is one nurse to every 250 to 300 new families. At this ratio it is not a timely personal relationship.

This support system should be reinforced and supple-mented with parenting classes and networks for all parents. The benefit here would come from the provision of information and creating for the mothers an informal support group of peers. Many middle class mothers make use of the National Childbirth Trust (NCT) sessions and go on to form tight bonds with other mums being similarly smitten and tested by their babies.

Mellow Parenting and Parent Network Scotland both provide group-coaching sessions for 'Bumps' during pregnancy and for parents after birth. Parent Network Scotland runs Parenting Matters at £175 per person for an eight-week session. Assuming participation by two parents for all of Scotland's 54,000 babies born in a year in such a programme this would cost £9.45 million.

It's also sensible to build comprehensive parenting preparation into the first hospital visit during pregnancy or into the process for receiving a Baby Box.

The point is – if there is the will there is a way of making real progress rapidly in today's Scotland.

■ Toddlers

Some children at two years of age will already carry the toll of adverse experiences. Voluntary organisations like With Kids in the east end of Glasgow specialise in play therapy while providing practical support for parents and carers.

Community-based play centres like Olivebank in East Lothian work with a small number of children and parents who are struggling to keep their children from going into care. Olivebank manages on a budget of £500,000 a year in its work with 50 children and their parents. Scaling this up across Scotland, working on population count and not factoring in increased disadvantage, would cost £51 million.

Across Scotland there are many excellent empathetic people working with young children. But in Holland, Germany and many European countries they go further than us and have a highly trained workforce that specialises in working with young children. These workers are known as pedagogues. They are trained to a Higher National Certificate, Higher National Diploma and degree level in behavioural science, working with young children, dealing with conflict and promoting team work. Day care staff should have the time, authority and skills to provide constructive feedback to parents.

I have been unable to arrive at a national cost to provide the Dutch support system of a family Mother and Baby Well-being Clinic and a family worker to each of our one in four most troubled parents. There are too many 'depends', as in depends on how many health visitors we have. As we saw in Chapter Three in Dunedin, New Zealand, they found that 22% of the adults at 38 years of age were responsible for the vast majority of poor outcomes from criminal convictions, to use of prescriptions, to benefit uptake, to hospital nights. A test that took 45 minutes to administer at age three was able to predict with 80% accuracy the people most likely to have a disadvantaged life and present the greatest burden to the public services. If we tackled this big issue earlier, and achieved a useful reduction in the number of 'at risk' children by the age of three, there would be substantial reductions in cost across health, social services, law enforcement, prison system and education.

Of course this road map can and must be improved upon. What it provides more than anything else is a sense of direction. All the science and data in this book would not be worth a jot if Scotland continued to accept 'what is for you will not go by you' for each of those maternity ward children.

The principles and the players

There are some principles that we need to embed into our behaviour as parents, as a culture and in government.

Firstly, and simply, Children Come First. In our thinking and behaviour, individually and as a society, our decisions and actions should always take account of the likely impact on our children, whether they are still in the womb or are heading out to school. Child well-being and the rights of children ought to be a national priority in the way that it is for the countries at the top of the UNICEF league table.

Secondly, the buck must stop with parents. Not government. Not 'society'. Not the police, not social work and not schools or GPs. The quest is to help parents, especially first-timers and those who have already suffered from the ignorance or worse of their own parents to be better prepared to have children and do a decent job in bringing them up.

Projects, initiatives and services are needed to support, coach and mentor parents across the spectrum of need. Some families can rely on their own stability and natural instincts but need help with specifics like feeding or sleep patterns. Other families need a significant and prolonged intervention to make a major transition away from inadequate or destructive behaviour.

Thirdly, government does of course have a substantial role to play in supporting parents to do the best possible job. As a principle we should require that our major state institutions re-evaluate their strategies, budgets and what they do through the prism of their impact on children, our most vulnerable members of society. The same subsidies made available for childcare should be offered to parents who decide to look after their own young children.

Fourthly, as we learned from other European countries, enlightened employment practices play a major role in enabling parents to invest precious time in building the closest relationships with their children. Some of this comes of course from government legislation but, as a principle, we need to find ways of embedding a different employment culture within organisations, both in the private and public sectors.

Fifth and finally, as we saw in the previous chapter, there is much good work being carried out by charities, civic organisations and in the public sector across our country to help children and parents. But it is scattered and on too small a scale. We should establish a fifth principle – that where good or best practice exists it should be built upon. Let's not reinvent the child well-being wheel.

But I would suggest one general rule – for our examples of what works we ought to look more often at our high scoring European neighbours and less at the US as it is 26th in the table of well-being.

■

Let's delve deeper into the four sets of players that would be involved in implementing the principles that I've outlined above. Each should check their values and the priority they give to parenting – parents, government, employers and civic society.

Parents have dilemmas to face, souls to search and priorities to realign. They have tough questions to ponder. Here are a few:

- ■ Have they prepared for pregnancy?

- ■ In our poor parenting culture, have they made the effort to become more knowledgeable?

- ■ Has their life-style adapted to the mother being pregnant?

- What ghosts rattle in their closet?

- Can they put their hands up and say 'We need help?'

- Has exhaustion created a self-control by-pass?

- Is more paid work genuinely for the benefit of the baby or is that just an excuse?

- Can parents relax in the knowledge that they have a handle on the child's well-being?

- Is parenting a joy or an extension of the cold war?

- Can they move to a three or four-day week – or will the employer still expect five days' output?

Potential and actual mothers and fathers need to be first understood as people and then as parents. Parent Network Scotland has an 'airplane oxygen mask' approach. In the safety drill before a plane takes off it is pointed out that if there is a sudden drop in pressure then parents should attach their own oxygen mask before trying to help their child. Parent Network Scotland knows from experience that they have to help parents get the 'oxygen' they need before turning to the child. In this way they can confront their own histories and circumstances and feel more competent and in control. For example it is not wise to expect a parent carrying a load of unresolved Adverse Childhood Experiences to sail effortlessly into parenthood.

In Holland it is easier to be a good parent, one at ease with the role because of the widespread skills and supportive cultural norms. In a previous chapter we encountered an American and a British woman who ended up being mothers in Holland. In their book they wrote: 'The Dutch have reined in the anxiety, stress and expectations of modern-day parenting, redefining the meaning of success and well-being. For them, success starts with happiness – that of their children and themselves.' From chocolate cake to preparing for pregnancy to tuning into children or being sensitive grandparents, behaviour is contagious.

Each family for good or bad contributes to the parenting culture. There is also an option to be publicly active. In another important way each of us has a sphere of influence. Some of that is in the family, in our job, who we know, what we talk about and do. Each of us has the licence, if we so choose to be proactive in our own family or in an extended circle of influence.

This calls for introspection fused with knowledge – recognising what we can do better in our own house or our own family or extended family to make the first 1,000 days and what follows as good as they can be.

But helping a family short of oxygen get the oxygen mask it needs means forming a trusting two-way relationship, building intimate knowledge and on some occasions intensive work over a long period of time. This is beyond the support on offer from any extended family: it is what Gerda, the family worker, did in Holland, forming a clear plan for the mother and children and giving support until they could look after themselves. It's where government comes in.

Government initiatives frequently appear like fashion items, here today gone tomorrow. But if we are to make children and their parenting a national priority followed through for ten to 50 years so that it takes root and becomes the new norm, we need the state to steer in a different direction and then solidly keep on track.

A junior Early Years Minister, however enthusiastic, does not carry the weight to make changes that need to be made in health, education and at arm's length in local government.

Government and politicians will not, I suspect, move much ahead of public opinion. What people want and what governments do overlap. The more that a broad sweep of people are concerned and the more the chattering classes chat, the more likely politicians will act. The more that government shows that it is willing to be proactive and serious – the more likely public opinion will change and institutions will recalibrate what they do. The virtuous circle will begin to spin.

After parents and government, **public organisations and private employers** are the third player. Employers from FTSE 100 companies to local authorities, family businesses and professional firms have values and cultures that directly affect parents. There are laws on maternity and paternity leave and then there is practice. Can the option of flexible or part-time work be made available for pregnant women and the parents of babies? Does it count against you if you leave the workplace to care for your child? If you do go part-time, say down to four days – do you still have five days' work to do in one week?

In the UK 54% of legal and accounting jobs are filled by women. Do firms know how to support and win the long- term commitment of their young women and men? Big corporations have glowing human resource statements. But only 41 companies and public organisations (none of which is registered in Scotland) have signed up to The Working Mums Employers' Charter, 'as a statement of their commitment to embracing the business case for flexible working, and enabling parents to progress and enhance their careers'.

As we have seen, in Holland it is the norm for employees to leave work when they have more important child commitments. Part-time working is endemic: three out of four women and one in four men follow this growing practice. Even more importantly there is a culture across all employers that 'the job' must not be their people's be-all-and-end-all. Children and family responsibilities come first – or at least have considerably more weight than in Scotland.

What steps do we have to take to embed such revolutionary cultures and practices into Scottish employment? Big ones, that's for sure, probably starting with companies looking at their own longer-term interests as the proportion of women grows in senior professional and management jobs. Government legislation and encouragement through trade bodies would help. It is going to be difficult to separate our working culture from the consumerism of the job-obsessed Americans who score so badly in that telling UNICEF table.

Civic and voluntary organisations are the fourth player. They already do much. But for some organisations there is a need to take stock and see if their values and what they do adequately reflects the needs of parents.

Can they find enough wiggle room to look afresh at what they are trying to do and how they operate? When I was at the Wise Group I tried to extend the help we were giving to the long-term unemployed people who were also parents.

A similar rethink could apply to organisations that focus on mental health or say, food banks: can their definition of what they do, how they frame their work, be shifted? Too often people are boxed in a single condition – 'Homeless', 'Out of Work', and 'Mental Health Problem'. What about 'Parent'?

But around the country we can find telling case studies of imagination and enterprise being used by people in civic and public life. For example, I watched a primary school head teacher's face light up when she explained how her school in Blairgowrie had been transformed. They found more and more ways of working with parents before their children came to school. They teamed up with parents who were struggling badly, helped them make soup and other simple meals, in the process building up trust and creating an influential relationship with mums and sometimes fathers.

It needs thought and it means moving onto the front foot. Not easy in the pell-mell of targets, reporting and rules that accompany public sector jobs. But it does demonstrate the potential for personal initiative and, perhaps, some creative initiatives by the public sector bodies that work closely with parents and children.

Some FAQs (frequently asked questions)
1. Isn't this just too big a challenge for our wee country to tackle?

Today we take clean water for granted. The early Victorians did not. Frequent outbreaks of typhoid and cholera in Glasgow disappeared when in 1859 Queen Victoria opened the Loch Katrine reservoir and supporting aqueducts. Fifty million gallons of clean water a day flowed on the 34-mile journey through rock and hillside to Glasgow – subsequent additions have added a further 40 million gallons a day. Making do with what they had was not good enough for the Victorians: their world was changing too rapidly.

Other major advances have been made. In 1960 25 children in every 1,000 live births in Scotland died before the age of one. By 2015 there was a fivefold improvement with just less than five children in every 1,000 births dying before the age of one. There is room for improvement but largely children survive. The challenge is now to ensure that they also thrive. Public health is as much about having good parents as clean water.

Talking of public health initiatives, we should also recall the marked success of a more recent project to tackle another peculiarly societal problem in Scotland – knife crime. Back in 2005 a United Nations study labelled us as the most violent country in the developed world. Scots were apparently three times as likely to be assaulted as Americans, and 30 times more likely than the Japanese. In the five years following that study a total of 40 children and teenagers were killed by knife attack in Scotland.

But in 2005 Strathclyde Police set up its Violence Reduction Unit to tackle the menace of the blade, with particular reference to Glasgow where the problem was greatest. Rather than use conventional policing methods, the force involved health, education and social work services in an integrated public health initiative to tackle attitudes and behaviour.

Much has been written about this project, notably in former Detective Chief Superintendent and the Unit's co-director John Carnochan's Postcards book, *Conviction*, but suffice to say that in the five years to 2016 there were just eight knife-related deaths across Scotland – none in Glasgow. So we have 'previous' on confronting embedded mindsets and behaviours, particularly amongst Scotsmen.

According to the Early Development Indicator, a quarter of children arrive at primary school vulnerable on at least one count of emotional maturity, language and cognitive development, social competence, communication skills and physical health and well-being. The quest over the next ten to 50 years is to fully and deliberately prepare people to be supportive, responsible, committed and loving parents of young children.

Clean water, better parents: both are projects that take vision, values, time, commitment and an investment.

2. Aren't you just another advocate for the Nanny State?

Throughout this book I have framed the challenge as preparing parents and supporting parents. Parents can do this for themselves and the government and the voluntary sector can assist. In Holland and Finland parents welcome the approach I have outlined: a helping hand is what is needed in those lonely first 1,000 days strewn with health, feeding and sleeping problems and perhaps also personal crises.

In terms of scale, for me, the biggest abuses of rights are the following:

■ A child being removed from his or her parents' home by social workers.

■ A child being sexually abused, severely neglected or beaten up by the people who should be giving care.

■ Young men and women being locked up in young offender institutions and jail because of their poor time in the womb and/or their traumatised youth.

A new balance on rights has to be struck. One that comes down in favour of the yet-to-be-born and very young that are without a voice or the power to defend themselves.

In the past couple of years Scotland has been embroiled in a row about how far the Scottish Government should intervene in children's and families lives as a result of the 'named person' provision in the Children and Young People (Scotland) Act 2014. The Government, and various supporting charities, see it as a way to ensure that vulnerable children will not slip through the net. Opponents see the appointment of an official person to oversee the child's welfare and exchange information, as a 'snoopers' charter'. When the matter went to the Supreme Court judges did not oppose the intention behind the bill but they said that as presently framed it breached privacy and family rights. The named person scheme continues to be dogged by controversy and is losing many MSPs' support.

What is interesting is that Highland Council have been using a named person procedure for years without controversy. Social workers in the region thought it was working well and helping to protect vulnerable children. If the Scottish Government had simply encouraged other local authorities to follow suit this may not have led to opposition. The problem has resulted from the Government's desire to enshrine this approach in legislation. Many see this as heavy-handed.

The Scottish Government's desire for a named person's procedure, and the resultant opposition, illustrates an important point. In Scandinavia and other European countries, people see the state as benign and enabling. Not so in Scotland. We often see it as centralising, dictatorial and acting in its own interest, not ours. This means that the measures I am suggesting in this book must be understood and supported by Scottish citizens. It is ordinary people themselves who must be seen to drive these changes. If any government's actions are too much ahead of public opinion then people will object vehemently.

3. How much will it cost to implement all this – and how can we afford it?

Let's look at the big picture to see where child-care and early years fit in to governmental priorities. The Scottish Government's draft budget for 2017/18 was £38.2 billion.

Of the £3.4 billion that goes to education and skills, £167 million will be spent on Children and Families. For a comparison that's one-sixteenth of the £2.67 billion that goes to the Scottish Funding Council (mainly for universities) and Higher Education Student Support.

Health expenditure amounts to £13.2 billion. A very small slice of the £9.3 billion for local health boards will go towards pregnancies, parents and babies. A budget line of £49.6 million is identified for Early Years – this includes spending on health visitors and IVF.

Between Education and Health budgets the dedicated money to early years totals £216 million. That's 0.56% of our national budget, or two-thirds of the amount spent on Scottish prisons.

For 2017/18 the overall budget had the following items:

- Concessionary Fares and bus services £254m
- Motorway and trunk roads £967m
- Rail Services £775m
- Prisons £361m

Infrastructure and investment is focused on motorways, rail services and prisons. Is it right that we spend the largest chunk of our education budget on universities and colleges, rather than on our youngest 'students'? Why do we ignore Heckman's rate of return on benefits gained and burdens avoided – being greatest right at the start? Is it sensible that our health spending is distorted to prolonging the lives of our oldest people instead of enriching the well-being of our youngest? And why in the welfare budget is the largest cost, state pensions, protected while Working Family Tax Credits that go to the lowest-earning parents and children are being reduced? Given the scale of the mismatch, tolerating children almost seems an over-generous description.

A start would be for the current UK and Scottish Government to become transparent on how much they spend per head on say a six-month-old, a 20 year-old and an 80 year-old?

What would it take to put in place a preventative health and social service system? The Kilbrandon Report originally suggested this. In 1964 it made two recommendations: the establishment of Children's Panels, which came to pass, and the setting up across all local authorities of a therapeutic and support service for children and parents at risk. This was rejected. In 2011 the Christie Commission recommended reform of public services towards prevention. It hasn't happened.

Here I have recommended the Dutch system of one family-one plan, with someone like Gerda immersing herself in the family, coaching and being a ringmaster for the different services. I cannot work out a cost for this service; there are too many variables. I know it would be a substantial investment, but over time it would also bring a substantial rate of return.

To be provocative, why don't we think about redirecting money in the budget and investing just 1% of the Scottish

Government's £38.2bn budget in an expansion (not a clever representation of figures) of the approach outlined above? What could they do with that £382 million? Quite a lot.

4. What are the chances of the Scottish Government actually playing its part in such a huge, ambitious, long-term quest?

The first thing to say is that the Scottish Government and parliament have been more active in their commitment to improving child well-being than the Westminster Government. It would be miserly not to recognise that in times of reduced public sector budgets a lot has been done to preserve and improve services aimed at supporting children and parents.

To fully answer the question, we should examine the Scottish Government's track record to date.

First, health visitors: these are well-accepted solid professional people trained in assessing the needs of mothers and young children. They judge whether a gentle hand on the shoulder might be enough, or if the mother's mental state has crumbled and there is no one else to help. They know too that adults can put on a brave face and hide what they do not want to be seen.

Cinderella and health visitors have much more in common than we think. Both have suffered low status and neglect. Morale has been low and the age profile has become older and older as early retirement with a pension became a sunny option.

In England the health visitor service continues to be neglected, money is coming out rather than going in and morale is low. But in Scotland health visitors have now been invited to the ball. The plan and money is now there to increase the workforce of just over 1,000 by a further 500 by 2018. But from what I can tell most mothers still only see a health visitor three times after birth and that is it. The plan, a reinvigorated pathway for mothers and babies, is good. It starts in pregnancy and the health visitor is scheduled to make eleven home visits. A development and well-being review is planned when the baby is between 13 and 15 months and again between 27 and 30 months. For this new pathway to be an effective preventative and early intervention programme, benefiting the mother and the baby, two preconditions need to be met. First, if at the development and well-being review, issues of concern are identified then back-up services will need to be there and able to act with urgency. Second, a clear financial commitment is needed to supporting the health visitor expansion programme. At the time of writing neither the Scottish Government nor the NHS have made this financial commitment.

Health visitors are there to promote good health, prevent problems blowing up, identify issues early and step in to directly help or pull in other people. When it works well, as it often does, trust is built up, a relationship created and there is less reason or opportunity for parents to hide. Remember that what is important gets measured so having formal assessments on well-being and development and acting on the results at this early formative stage makes a big difference.

An extra 500 health visitors may not be enough to empower Scottish mothers and fathers but it takes us in the right direction. A statutory role for health visitors protects parents and tees up the service for a more substantial role. However a caseload for each health visitor of between 250 and 300 new babies and their carers is unrealistic if support is to be personal and timely.

The Scottish Government also showed leadership in 2012 in creating the Early Years Collaborative. This introduced a series of stretch targets across 32 Local Authorities, 14 regional health boards, 14 local policing divisions and innumerable voluntary organisations. The Early Years Collaborative brought thousands of people together across the country to inspire one another, improve methods and assist cross-service working.

For some reason, it has been allowed to wither or go dormant – perhaps it has been sidelined because the quantitative targets set were rushed into and a bit wonky; or it is just another fashion victim? Steps are being taken to improve child protection and care for children removed from their parental homes. More support has been directed to some pregnant teenagers through the Family Nurse Partnership. A Child Poverty Bill was approved in 2017 and a Minister for Child Care and Early Years has been created in the Scottish Government.

On its intent to do the right thing the Scottish Government scores highly. It has expanded day care for three and four-year-olds and more disadvantaged two-year-olds. However, in practice this good intent is badly targeted or framed. The biggest issue in Scotland is how parents prepare for having a child and a healthy pregnancy and the relationship between the parents and the child. All of this is way before a parent ever crosses the door of a nursery. A clearer sense of purpose is needed and a scale of commitment to match the task at hand: one in four children reaches primary school disadvantaged.

Baby Boxes are a material way of helping parents prepare for a newborn baby. However in Scotland the midwife fills in the form and a number of weeks later, near the end of the pregnancy the Baby Box is delivered. In Finland, where the idea came from, parents collect the box from the maternity and child health clinic before the birth of their child. It is a gift from the community but also a way of strengthening the link with support services during pregnancy and building on the sense of rights and responsibilities. A box of stuff from the postman – however well meaning – is no substitute for supportive relationships. I hope the evaluation of the Baby Boxes will take this into account.

The Scottish Government has had a National Parenting Strategy for the past five years. This is welcome. But a good strategy document, few powers, little authority and a small budget do not measure up to the task in hand. Getting it Right for Every Child is strong on the rights of children and has created a framework that has helped local decision makers. To move up the child well-being league requires an appropriately sized budget and authority. It is time to break with the Implementation Deficit Syndrome.

Vision
We need a vision to serve as an inspiration and a beacon, to set direction along the rocky and joyous road over the coming years and decades. Here is mine.

In the foreseeable future I want us to become a country where regard and respect is given to the first 1,000 days. I want all the babies born in the maternity ward to have a better life. Not necessarily a perfect life but a better life. And when the time comes for them to have children, I want their children to have even better life chances.

Shared vision helps to bind us together and create a personal and national purpose. The critical indicator of a successful

Scotland should be how all children are nurtured so that they become adults that can stand on their own feet and thrive. This is our collective responsibility.

The numbers reveal the opportunity. In the next five years over 250,000 babies will be born in Scotland. This means that a sizeable number of people will become new parents. When we consider the benefits of investing early in these parents and babies we see what an important issue this is not just for them but for Scotland. The future happiness and quality of life for of an awful lot of Scots hangs on what we achieve together in the next few years in cultivating child well-being. How well our society functions, and the health of Scotland, also hangs in this balance.

Let me conclude by pharaphrasing Nelson Mandela: 'There is no keener revelation of Scotland's soul than the way it prepares for and treats its children'.

THE END

Key references

This is a list of key references for each chapter. For a fuller set of references, live internet links to reports, journal articles etc listed below go to
www.postcardsfromscotland.co.uk/book14.htm

Chapter One: Introduction

BENTLEY, H., et al., 2017. *How safe are our children? The most comprehensive overview of child protection in the UK.* NSPCC

CENTRE ON THE DEVELOPING CHILD, Harvard University, 2017. *InBrief: Early Childhood Mental Health.* Cambridge: Harvard University

CENTRE ON THE DEVELOPING CHILD, Harvard University, 2017. *InBrief: The Foundations of Lifelong Health.* (Online video). Cambridge: Harvard University NSPCC, 2018

WOLFSON L., et al., 2013. A cross sectional pilot study of the Scottish early development instrument: a tool for addressing inequality. *BMC Public Health*, 2013 13:1187.

Chapter Two: An epiphany

CENTRE ON THE DEVELOPING CHILD, Harvard University, 2016. *Building Core Capabilities for Life: The Science Behind the Skills Adults Need to Succeed in Parenting and the Workplace.* Cambridge: Harvard University

SCOTTISH ENTERPRISE, 2005. *Future Skills Scotland. Voluntary Scottish Sector Profile*

SINCLAIR, A., 2007. 0-5: How Small Children Make a Big Difference. *The Work Foundation Provocation Series Volume 3 Number 1.* London: The Work Foundation

Chapter Three: What science and research tells us about the early years

AUDIT SCOTLAND, 2010. *Getting it right for children in residential care*

BRADSHAW, P., 2011. *Growing Up in Scotland: Changes in child cognitive ability in the pre-school years*. Edinburgh: Scottish Government

BROMLEY, C., & CUNNINGHAM-BURLEY, S., 2010. *Growing Up in Scotland: Health inequalities in the early years.* Edinburgh: Scottish Government

CASPI, A., et al., 2016. Childhood forecasting of a small segment of the population with large economic burden. *Nature Human Behaviour* Volume 1

GEDDES, R., HAW, S., FRANK, J., 2010. *Interventions for Promoting Early Child Development for Health: An environmental scan with special reference to Scotland*. Edinburgh: Scottish Collaboration for Public Health Research and Policy

GLASGOW CITY COUNCIL, Glasgow City Integrated Joint Board, 8 November 2017, Item No. 6

HECKMAN, J. J., et al., 2010. The Rate of Return to the High Scope Perry Preschool Program. *Journal of Public Economics*, Volume 94, Issues 1–2, February 2010, pp. 114-128

HIGHSCOPE, 2018. *Perry Preschool Study*, (website) https://highscope.org/perrypreschoolstudy

MILLER, S, 2017. *Item No. 6 – Transformational Change Programme – Children's Services 2018-21.* Glasgow City Integrated Joint Board, 8th November 2017.

PERRY, B. D., & SZALAVITZ, M., 2006. *The Boy Who Was Raised as a Dog: And Other Stories from a Child Psychiatrist's Notebook – What Traumatized Children Can Teach Us About Loss, Love, and Healing.* New York: Basic Books

POULTON, R., MOFFITT T. E., & Silva, P. A., 2015. The Dunedin Multidisciplinary Health and Development Study: Overview of the first 40 years with an eye to the future. *Social Psychiatry and Psychiatric Epidemiology*, 2015 50:679–693

SCOTTISH GOVERNMENT, 2017. Table 1.1: Number of children looked after by type of accommodation (Table). In: *Children's Social Work Statistics Scotland 2015/16.*

UNIVERSITY OF OTAGO, 2016. *2016 Winter Lecture – The Dunedin Longitudinal Study: Superb Science, but so what?* (Online video)

Chapter Four: In Scotland we tolerate children

ACOSTA, R., M., & HUTCHISON, M., 2017. *The Happiest Kids in the World: Building up children in the Dutch way*. London: Penguin Random House

ADAMSON, P., 2013. *UNICEF Office of Research. Report Card 11: Child Well-being in rich countries*. Florence: UNICEF Office of Research – Innocenti

FAMILY PLANNING ASSOCIATION 2010. *Teenage Pregnancy Fact Sheet*. London: Family Planning Association

INFORMATION SERVICES DIVISION PUBLICATION REPORT, 2017. *Teenage Pregnancy* Year of conception ending 31 December 2015

IPSOS MORI & NAIRN, A., 2011. *Children's Well-being in the UK, Sweden and Spain: The Role of Inequality and Materialism*

McGARVEY, D., 2017. *Poverty Safari: Understanding the Anger of Britain's Underclass*. Edinburgh: Luath Press Ltd

SINCLAIR, A., 2011. *Early Years and Transformational Change, Churchill Travelling Fellowship Report*. Glasgow: Centre for Confidence and Well-being

ISD SCOTLAND, (Website) 2017, *Teenage Pregnancy: Maternity and Births.*

Chapter Five: Before birth

BRADFORD, E., 2015. Drinking in Pregnancy 'Significant' Cause of Brain Damage in Children. BBC Online News 23rd June 2015

BRADSHAW, P., et al, 2013. *Growing Up in Scotland: Birth Cohort 2 – Results from the first year*. Edinburgh: Scottish Government

CENTER FOR DISEASE CONTROL AND PREVENTION, (Website) 2017. *Preconception health and health care*.

CENTRE ON THE DEVELOPING CHILD, Harvard University, 2017a. *InBrief: Early Childhood Mental Health*. Cambridge: Harvard University

CENTRE ON THE DEVELOPING CHILD, Harvard University, 2017b. *InBrief: The Foundations of Lifelong Health*. (Online video). Cambridge: Harvard University

CENTRE ON THE DEVELOPING CHILD, Harvard University,

2017c. *InBrief: The Science of Early Childhood Development.* Cambridge: Harvard University.

FORD, K., 2014. Understanding the use of alcohol in Pregnancy amongst Scottish Women. *Knowledge Transfer Publication Series: Economic and Social Research Council and the Scottish Government Joint PhD Scheme*

GLOVER, V., & SUTTON, C., 2012. Support from the start: effective programmes in pregnancy. *Journal of Children's Services*, Vol 7 No 1, pp8-17

LEE, K. K., et al., 2015. Maternal Obesity During Pregnancy Associates with Premature Mortality and Major Cardiovascular Events in Later Life. Hypertension 2015;66:938-944

NATIONAL GEOGRAPHIC, (Video), 2005. *In the Womb.*

NHS CHOICES, 2015. *Your Pregnancy and Baby Guide. Domestic Abuse*

O'HAGAN, A., et al, 2013. *Equalities Scottish Government Equality Outcomes: Pregnancy and Maternity Evidence Review.* Edinburgh: Scottish Government

SHER, J., 2016. *Missed Periods: Scotland's Opportunities for Better Pregnancies.* Glasgow: NHS Greater Glasgow and Clyde (Public Health)

SCOTTISH GOVERNMENT, 2015. *Tackling inequalities in the early years: Key messages from 10 years of the Growing Up in Scotland study* Edinburgh: The Scottish Government

SCOTTISH GOVERNMENT. Table 5; Charts 3, 4. In: *Homicide in Scotland 2016-17.* Edinburgh: Scottish Government

SHONKOFF, J. P., PHILLIPS, D. A., Eds. 2000. *From Neurons to Neighborhoods: The Science of Early Childhood Development.* Washington: National Academy Press

Chapter 6 Those first two vital years of life

CARNOCHAN, J., 2015. *Conviction.* Edinburgh: Argyll Publishing

HARLOW, H., 1958. The Nature of Love. *American Psychologist*, 13, 573-685.

HRDY, S. B., 1999. *Mother Nature: Natural Selection and the Female of the Species,.* London: Chatto & Windus

KILDAY, A., 2013. *A History of Infanticide in Britain c. 1600 to the Present.* London: Palgrave School

McANDREW, F., et al. 2010. *Infant Feeding Survey 2010*. London: The Health and Social Care Information Centre. NHS CHOICES, (website), 2017. *Benefits of Breastfeeding.*

NHS INFORMATION SERVICES DIVISION, 2016. *Breastfeeding Statistics Scotland*.

PERRY, B. D. & HAMBRICK, E., 2008. The Neurosequential Model of Therapeutics. *Reclaiming Children and Youth*, v17 n3 p38-43 Fall 2008. Available from: https://eric.ed.gov/ ?id=EJ869926 (Accessed January 2018)

ROLLINS, N. C., et al., 2016. Why invest, and what will it take to improve breastfeeding practices? *The Lancet* Volume 387, No. 10017, pp. 491–504, 30th January 2016.

TheSasss1, 2012. *Harlow's Monkeys*. (Online video). Available at: https://www.youtube.com/watch?v=_O60TYAIgC4

VICTORIA, C. G., et al., 2016. Breastfeeding in the 21st century: epidemiology, mechanisms, and lifelong effects. *The Lancet* 2016, Volume 387, No. 10017, p475–490, 30 January 2016

ZEEDYK, S., 2014. *Sabre Tooth Tigers & Teddy Bears: the connected baby guide to understanding attachment* (Online).

Chapter 7 Is social class a factor?

BELLIS, A. M., et al. 2015. *Welsh Adverse Childhood Experiences (ACE) Study. Adverse Childhood Experiences and their Impact on Health-harming Behaviours in the Welsh Adult Population*. Cardiff: Public Health Wales

COUPER, S. et al., 2016. *'Polishing the Diamonds': Addressing Adverse Childhood Experiences in Scotland*. Glasgow: Scottish Public Health Network.

DUFFELL, N., 2014. *Wounded Leaders: the Psychohistory of British Elitism and the Entitlement Illusion*. London: Lone Arrow Press

FELITTI, V. J., et al. 1998. Relationship of Childhood Abuse and Household Dysfunction to Many of the Leading Causes of Death in Adults. *American Journal of Preventive Medicine*, Volume 14, Issue 4, pp. 245-258.

LEVINE, M., 2006. *The Price of Privilege: How Parental Pressure and Material Advantage are Creating a Generation of Disconnected and Unhappy Kids*. New York: Harper

MARRYAT, L. et al., [no date]. *The prevalence of ACEs in the general population of Scottish children in the first eight years of life.* (Available on request from: louise.marryat@ed.ac.uk)

RENTON, A., 2017. *Stiff Upper Lip: Secrets, Crimes and the Schooling of a Ruling Class.* London: Weidenfeld &Nicolson.

ROSIN, H., 2015. The Silicon Valley Suicides. *The Atlantic,* December 2015.

SELZER, F.L., 2015. *This is What Really Makes Narcissists Tick.* [Online]. Psychology Today.

SCOTTISH GOVERNMENT, 2015. *Tackling inequalities in the early years: Key messages from 10 years of the Growing Up in Scotland study* Edinburgh: The Scottish Government.

SCOTTISH GOVERNMENT, 2017. *Poverty and Income Inequality in Scotland: 2015/16.*

VINER, R. et al, 2017. *State of Child Health Report,* Royal College of Paediatrics and Child Health.

WOLFSON L., et al., 2013. A cross sectional pilot study of the Scottish early development instrument: a tool for addressing inequality. *BMC Public Health*, 2013 13:1187.

Chapter 8 Crisis is the time to change direction

BOYLE, S., 2016, *The Stanford Marshmallow Experiment and the Scottish Economy*, Glasgow: *The Herald*

COYLE, D. et al., 2005, *New Wealth for Old Nations*, Princeton University Press

O'DONNELL, G., 2017. *In Pursuit of Wellbeing*, Gus O'Donnell, London: Royal Society of the Arts Journal

KAHNEMAN, D., 2011.*Thinking, Fast and Slow,* London: Penguin Books

Measurement of the Extent of Youth Crime in Scotland, Scottish Government March 2015.

SCOTTISH GOVERNMENT, 2008. *Shifting the Balance of Care*, Scottish Government

The International Monetary Fund, 2009.*The Fiscal Implications of the Global Economic and Financial Crisis*, Occasional Paper 269

www. Heckmanequation.org

Chapter 9 Optimism

FAMILY NURSE PARTNERSHIP,
    www.scottishgovernment/familynursepartnership

FRAIBERG S. et al.,1975. *Ghosts in the Nursery: A Psychoanalytic Approach to the Problems of Impaired Infant-Mother Relationships*, Child and Adolescent Psychiatry

NSPCC, 2016. *Looking After Infant Mental Health: Our Case for Change: A summary of research evidence*, NSPCC

SYLVA, K., et al., 2014, *Student's educational and development outcomes at age 16, Effective Pre-school, Primary and Secondary Education (EPPSE 3-16) Project*, Department of Education

WEIL, G. and MARDEN,D.,2009,. Teach Yourself *Bringing Happy Children*, New York: McGraw-Hill

THE SCOTTISH GOVERNMENT,2015. Universal Health Visiting Pathway in Scotland: Pre-Birth to Pre-School

UNISON SCOTLAND, 2016. *Health Visitor Survey*

Chapter 10 A road map to better child well-being

AUDIT SCOTLAND, 2010, Getting it right for children in residential care

AVSHALOM,C., et al., 2016. *Childhood forecasting of a small segment of the population with large economic burden*, Nature Human Behaviour

COVEY,S.C. , 1997, *The 7 Habits of Highly Effective Families*, Golden Books

McFADDEN, A., et al, 2015. *Breastfeeding: Policy Matters*, Save the Children

ROSENBERG, M.B., 2005. *Raising Children Compassionately*, Encinitas USA: Puddle Dancer Press

SCOTTISH GOVERNMENT, 2017/18. *Draft Budget, Level 3*

THE HEALTH FOUNDATION, 2017. Infant Mortality, Quality Watch

Coaching and courses on parenting in Scotland and excellent materials are available from:

Mellow Parenting http://www.mellowparenting.org

Scottish Attachment in Action https://www.saia.org.uk

Parenting Network Scotland – Parenting Matters Course http://www.parentnetworkscotland.org.uk

Acknowledgements

If you are still reading the book at this stage then it is down to the work of Alastair Balfour. As the editor he has encouraged, engaged, dug me out of holes and made the whole text more readable. Carol Craig has worked hard to publish this book and over the years presented ideas and sympathetically listened and discussed many of the book's topics. Babies and books both need helpful people.

W isdom and generosity have been shown by a group of readers: Glenys Watt, John Frank, Eden Anderson, Tam Baillie, Edwina Grant, Matt Forde, Susan Sinclair, Mike Burns, Gillian Gierthy, Stephen Boyle and Chris Palmer. Jonathan Sher read, commented and helped me work through some tricky issues. At an earlier stage Paul Gierthy and Charlie Woods offered sage advice. Professor John Russell provided guidance on the weeks before and after birth. I would like to thank them all for their support.

I would also like to thank Rhiannon Van Muysen for providing a sensitive piece of art for the front cover.

Over the last ten years I have been entrusted with many personal stories. I would like to thank each person for allowing me to relate what I have been told. In some places I have tweaked names and locations to preserve confidences.

I have attempted to make clear complex findings and

theories across a range of disciplines. My gratitude goes to the people who for years have done the hard work in conducting experiments, analysing data and thinking hard about their area of expertise.

Any bungling and mistakes are mine.

Michele Veldman my wife has been patient and supportive. Eva and Thomas have given inspiration. Millie our dog has no sense of delayed gratification and made sure I had regular walks. I want to thank you for reading this book and if you see fit passing it on.

Alan Sinclair
February 2018

Other books in the series

1. AfterNow – What next for a healthy Scotland?
| *Phil Hanlon/Sandra Carlisle*
The authors of this visionary book look at health in Scotland
and beyond health to the main social, economic,
environmental and cultural challenges of our times. They
examine the type of transformational change required to create
a more resilient and healthy Scotland.

2. The Great Takeover – How materialism, the media and
markets now dominate our lives | *Carol Craig*
Describes the dominance of materalist values, the media and
business in all our lives and how this is leading to a loss of
individual and collective well-being. It looks at many of the big
issues of our times – debt, inequality, political apathy, loss of
self-esteem, pornography and the rise of celebrity culture. The
conclusion is simple and ultimately hopeful – we can change
our values and our lives.

3. The New Road – Charting Scotland's inspirational
communities | *Alf Young / Ewan Young*
A father and son go on a week long journey round Scotland to
see at first hand some of the great environmental, social,
employment and regeneration projects which are happening.
From Dunbar in the south east of Scotland to Knoydart in the
north west they meet people involved in projects which
demonstrate new ways of living.

4. Scotland's Local Food Revolution | *Mike Small*

Lifts the lid on the unsavoury reality of our current food system including horsemeat in processed beef products, the unsustainable movement of food round the globe, and how supermarket shopping generates massive waste. It's an indictment of a food syste that is out of control. But there is hope – the growth and strength of Scotland's local food movement.

5. Letting Go – Breathing new life into organisations | *Tony Miller/ Gordon Hall*

It is now commonplace for employees to feel frustrated at work – ground down by systems that are dominated by rules, protocols, guidelines, targets and inspections. Tony Miller and Gordon Hall explore the origins of 'command and control' management as well as the tyranny of modern day 'performance management'. Effective leaders, they argue, should 'let go' of their ideas on controlling staff and nurture intrinsic motivation instead.

6. Raising Spirits – Allotments, well-being and community | *Jenny Mollison/ Judy Wilkinson/ Rona Wilkinson*

Allotments are the unsung story of our times; hidden places for food, friendship and freedom from the conformity of everyday life. A fascinating look at how allotments came about; why they can make such a substantial contribution to health, well-being, community, food production, and the environment; and what's happening in other countries.

7. Schooling Scotland – Education, equity and community | *Daniel Murphy*

The Scottish schooling system does well for many children growing up in Scotland, but to ensure that all children get the education they deserve, a better partnership of parent, child, school, government and society is needed – one to which all Scotland can contribute and from which all children can benefit. Daniel Murphy suggests eight ways to ensure that Scottish education could be stronger and fairer.

8. Shaping our Global Future – A guide for young people | *Derek Brown*

Young people worry about the future world they will live in: personal futures, families and jobs. But they also worry about their global futures. The possibilities and challenges ahead appear overwhelming. This guide to human achievements and future challenges is designed to help young people consider the future their children and grandchildren will inhabit.

9. Conviction – Violence, culture and a shared public service agenda | *John Carnochan* Policeman John Carnochan takes us on a memorable journey of discovery as he comes to grips with violence and Scotland's traditionally high murder rate. He also gives a fascinating insight into the work of Scotland's Violence Reduction Unit and why it has been so spectacularly successful. This compelling book is not about high visibility policing or more officers but the importance of empathy and children's early years.

10. She, He, They – Families, gender and coping with transition | *Shirley Young*
How challenging can gender transition be for both parents and siblings? A story of hope and resilience, it shows that if parents can move beyond the shock and pain of their offspring's transition, all family members can come closer together and experience life-enhancing change.

11. Knowing and Growing – Insights for developing ourselves and others | *Alan McLean*
This extraordinary book provides insights and practical tools to help you navigate everyday human interactions, balance your own and others' needs and utilise your emotions to create a more fulfilling life. The powerful insights from 'McL ean's Ring' are not only helpful for parents, teachers and leaders they are also essential for anyone aiming to encourage others to grow and develop.

12. Working for Equality - Policy, politics people | Richard Freeman, Fiona McHardy, Danny Murphy (Editors) Brings together 22 experienced practitioners from across the country to reflect on equality/inequality – in class, race, gender, poverty, disability and homelessness as well as health and education. They are concerned about individuals as well as ideas and policy instruments. Short and accessible, a pause for thought and inspiration for those concerned with action.

More titles are planned for 2018.
Books can be ordered from www.postcardsfromscotland.co.uk or from www.amazon.co.uk Kindle editions are also available.

9780993352768
£10 in UK
Available now

Hiding in Plain Sight – exploring Scotland's ill health

no. 13 in the Postcards from Scotland series

Scotland. A country that prides itself on its modernity and progressive instincts. Yet this is a nation whose mental and physical health outcomes are poor by European standards. This book asks why?

Grippingly redable yet challenging, Carol Craig offers an answer which is glaringly obvious. Generations of Scottish children have suffered in ways that undermine the nation's health. Starting from her own and her neighbours' lives, she explores the growing awareness internationally of the impact of Adverse Childhood Experiences.

'hugely powerful, raw and brave'
Alistair Moffat, historian

'an important book. . . her compelling conclusions
are a challenge to us all'
Phil Hanlon, Emeritus Professor of Public Health